WELCOME

GREATEST SUPERBIKES OF ALL TIME

The rise of superbikes has been one of the defining stories of late 20th and early 21st century motorcycling. The fastest, most sophisticated, and dare I say 'sexiest' motorcycles of all, had never been clearly defined until Honda's first large capacity, multi-cylinder CB750 of 1969 was clearly so much more than just a 'bike', it had to be a 'superbike'.

And that, combined with the early 1970s emergence of a new production racing class for such 750s – F1 – which further fuelled the creation of such bikes, led to an all-new motorcycling era.

And what an era it was. The CB750 led to the Kawasaki Z1, which led to the Suzuki GS1000 then GSX, and so on. Suddenly four-cylinder Japanese 750s were not enough. Honda dabbled with V4s, Kawasaki redefined what was possible with its GPz900R, and Suzuki kick-started the 'racer replica' with the first GSX-R750.

Then things became more extreme still. The creation of the World Superbike Championship in 1988 made not only the superbike term official but was the catalyst for a whole new series of 750cc homologation special racers such as Honda's RC30 and made a star of Ducati's 916. The revision of world superbike regulations to allow 1000cc fours in 2003 then fuelled the ascendancy of bikes such as Suzuki's GSX-R1000, Aprilia's RSV4, and BMW's S1000RR.

All of these superbikes and more are revisited, explained and celebrated here, with behind-the-scenes back stories, unseen official pictures, and the statistics that made them special.

Everyone has a favourite superbike. I've ridden more than a few. Here are our best 50. ■

Phil West
Editor

BELOW: The Kawasaki GPZ900R – one of the finest bikes of the 1980s.

CONTENTS

GREATEST SUPERBIKES OF ALL TIME

1972 Kawasaki Z1

2018 Ducati Panigale V4

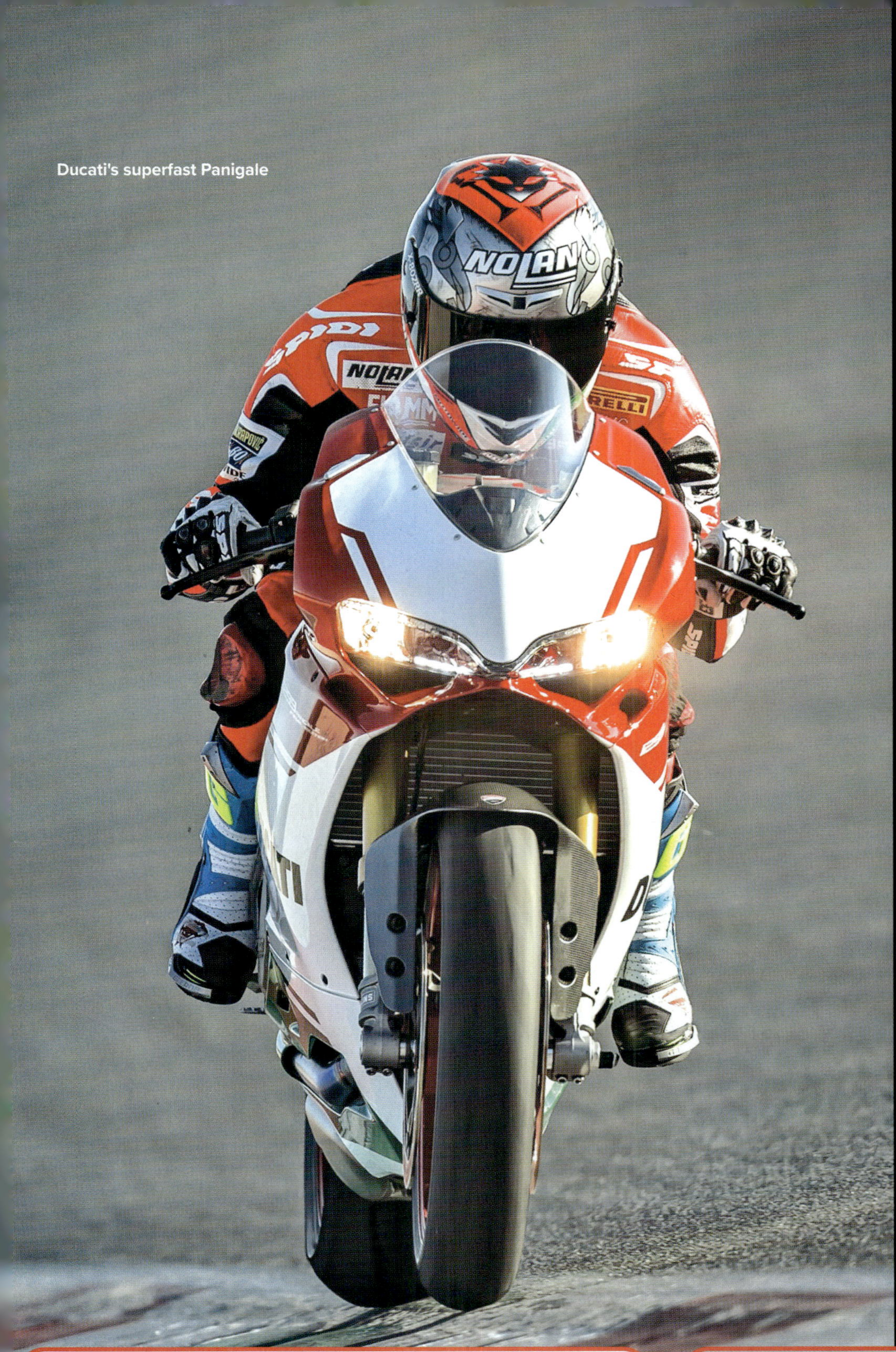

ISBN: 978 1 83632 197 2
Editor: Phil West
Senior editor, specials: Roger Mortimer
Email: roger.mortimer@keypublishing.com
Cover Design: Steve Donovan
Design: SJmagic DESIGN SERVICES, India
Advertising Sales Manager: Sam Clark
Email: sam.clark@keypublishing.com
Tel: 01780 755131
Advertising Production: Becky Antoniades
Email: Rebecca.antoniades@keypublishing.com

SUBSCRIPTION/MAIL ORDER
Key Publishing Ltd, PO Box 300,
Stamford, Lincs. PE9 1NA
Tel: 01780 480404
Subscriptions email: subs@keypublishing.com
Mail Order email: orders@keypublishing.com
Website: www.keypublishing.com/shop

PUBLISHING
Group CEO: Adrian Cox
Publisher: Steve O'Hara

Published by
Key Publishing Ltd, PO Box 100,
Stamford, Lincs. PE9 1XQ
Tel: 01780 755131
Website: www.keypublishing.com

PRINTING
Precision Colour Printing Ltd, Haldane,
Halesfield 1, Telford, Shropshire.
TF7 4QQ

DISTRIBUTION
Frontline Distribution Solutions Ltd,
2 Poultry Avenue, London, EC1A 9PU
Enquiries Line: 02074 294000.

1980 Suzuki GSX1100S Katana

1992 Honda CBR900RR FireBlade

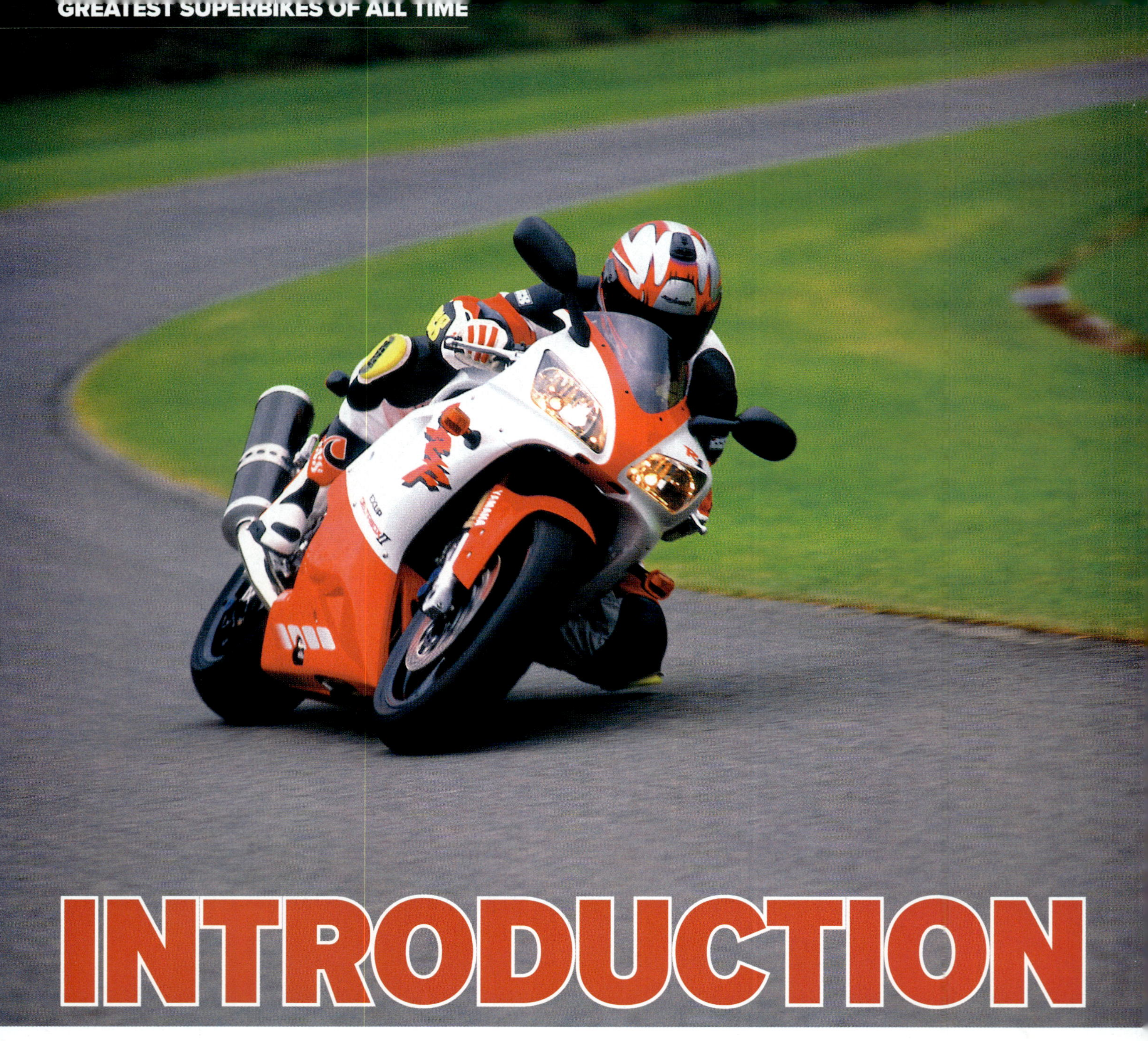

INTRODUCTION

What makes a superbike? Sometimes it's easier to define what isn't than what is. Is it capacity? The original superbike was the 1969 Honda CB750, yet today's Honda CB750, the twin cylinder Hornet, doesn't come close.

Is it performance? Not necessarily. Kawasaki's 1972 Z1 may have redefined motorcycle power with its 82bhp but today that power figure is virtually matched by the Japanese firm's 400cc ZX-4R which is by no measure a superbike.

Or is it style? With things like full fairings and premium cycle parts? After all, that's what qualified BMW's 1976 R100RS. Again, not really. BMW is still there. It's latest R1300RS has just the same recipe

but it would never be mistaken as a true superbike.

Instead, it's largely about the intangibles; about what they have been designed to achieve in their era, whether that's 'top performance dog' or specifically to be the best superbike racer of the time.

It's also about bringing something new to the party, about raising the performance bar, introducing new technologies, design principles, features or even style. And it's also, sometimes, about being a surprise, about delivering what previously wasn't thought possible (BMW's S1000RR and Kawasaki's 2015 Ninja H2 R immediately spring to mind here).

But the very best superbikes ever built – and hopefully we include all of

them here – qualify on all of the above counts, and even more besides.

Ducati's legendary 1994 916 is often touted as the best superbike of all time and it's difficult to argue against it. It was game changing, pioneering, from a historic manufacturer, was beautiful and had unparalleled success in the definitive superbike racing class – world superbikes. But there are others that can stake their own compelling claims.

Here are just a few of the 50 bikes we've rounded up in this special bookazine. How many can you recognise? Which ones are your favourites? Now read their full stories on the following pages. Maybe, when you've finished, your favourite won't be the 916 any more... ■

1968 TRIUMPH TRIDENT

Brilliant but flawed – the Brit triple that was very nearly the first superbike

Although Honda's game-changing CB750 four is often referred to as the first 'superbike', there is also an argument that Triumph's first three-cylinder Trident 750 (along with its sister bikes, the BSA Rocket3) should be awarded that mantle instead, as it beat – just – the Honda to market, was cheaper, in some ways better, and was also the first mass-market 750cc 'multi'.

Blighted by development delays, internal squabbles, production problems, dubious styling and quickly dated by its slow uptake of modern 'tech', such as disc brakes and an electric starter, the Trident is instead remembered most as a case of promise unfulfilled or as the bike that 'might have been'. True, subsequent versions were better looking and equipped, but by then it was too late: BSA had closed, Triumph was in turmoil, and the Japanese were racing ahead.

And yet it could all have been so different...

A Triumph triple had originally been considered as early as 1963, but the first prototype wasn't completed until 1965. The project was then paused due to internal politics until a meeting in 1966 where a sales executive revealed that Honda was working on a 750

four – and the Triumph triple was back on.

Trouble was, Triumph's then owners, BSA, decided that they, too, wanted their own version (which would become the Rocket3) and demanded that it be distinguished by its cylinders being canted forward 10°... and its own frame.

Soon after, the original, far simpler idea for a bike that 'looked like a Bonneville but with three cylinders' was dropped in favour of one with a look all its own. Ogle Design, which had been behind the Reliant Scimitar and later celebrated for the Raleigh Chopper and Bond Bug, were commissioned to deliver just that,

ABOVE: Initial styling by external design house Ogle, which had also been responsible for the Reliant Scimitar and Bond Bug cars, proved controversial.
PHIL WEST

BELOW: The British 'great white three-cylinder hope' had been conceived as early as 1965 but was delayed by political in-fighting, and design and production issues.
PHIL WEST

their designs took a further 18 months to complete and the Triumph triple, which could have revolutionised the world in 1965, finally arrived in 1968.

The three-cylinder engine was based on that of the Bonneville twin but with an extra cylinder. Dry sump with a 120° crank, the crankcases were in three parts with two camshafts running pushrods front and rear in traditional Triumph style. The cylinder head was a single casting, with two separate rocker boxes. The gearbox was originally a four-speeder with a right-hand change, and a single plate Borg and Beck clutch was also used. Early tests showed the Trident was much smoother than the 650 twin, but not much wider or heavier, produced 58bhp, and was considerably faster.

Much of the rest, was originally as per the Bonneville, including its duplex cradle frame, although, because of its single down tube, the Trident's middle exhaust split into two as it came out of the head, one to each of the outer downpipes.

Forks were similar to those of the twins, too, as was the front drum brake. The shock absorbers were shrouded, there was an oil tank on the right under a side panel, and a bank of three Amal Concentric Mk1 carbs.

The result, in its Ogle styling, was well received in the UK but the

SPECIFICATIONS

Price new	£895
Engine	740cc air-cooled in-line triple
Power	58bhp @ 7,250rpm
Torque	45lb-ft @ 6,900rpm
Frame	Tubular steel cradle
Suspension	Telescopic forks (F), twin shocks (R)
Brakes	8in TLS drum (F), 7in SLS drum (R)
Tyres	3.25 x 19 (F), 4.10 x 19 (R)
Dry weight	212kg
Top speed	125mph

US didn't like its styling at all, so much so that by 1970 it had been relaunched with a 1960s tank, new side panels and more conventional silencers, while BSA USA had commissioned what became the X75 Hurricane. Then, 1971 saw both versions get a restyle, fifth gear and disc brake.

By this point, however, Triumph/BSA production was in a mess. BSA stopped production of the Rocket3 that year, but Trident engines were made by BSA at Small Heath with frame and final assembly by Triumph at Meriden. When the Triumph workers blockade began at Meriden in the autumn of 1973, Trident production came to a halt and in order to resume, the new Norton Villiers Triumph company had to expensively retool Small Heath. As a result, no Tridents were made until 1974, by which time the kickstart-only Trident seemed obsolete next to the latest Japanese superbikes.

In 1975, a new version appeared, the T160, this time with the inclined BSA version of the engine but with a five-speed gearbox, new left-foot gearshift (to comply with new US regulations), the addition (at last) of an electric starter, disc brakes front and rear, new exhaust and, just as importantly, a whole new look. Finally, the Trident was the bike it always should have been.

Sadly, by then, recessions, oil prices, and increasingly modern competition meant that this final effort was also short-lived. Production at Small Heath culminated finally at year's end, although you could still buy a T160 into 1978 thanks to NVT selling a batch of triples left over from a cancelled order from the Saudi Arabian police as the 'Triumph Cardinal'.

By then, just 27,480 Trident/BSAs had been made. Over 500,000 Honda CB750s were produced over (roughly) the same period.

Although the Trident was a classic case of unfulfilled promise, it was never a bad bike. It even had significant success on track, most famously as 'Slippery Sam' winning five consecutive production TTs between 1971 and 1975. At the 1971 Daytona 200 (after infamously being beaten by Honda's CB750 the previous year), a Triumph/BSA team on Rob North-framed specials swept the podium. The same team, shortly after, inspired the creation of the Transatlantic Trophy.

All of that, plus the fact it was the last major motorcycle from Meriden Triumph, is enough for the Trident to have classic status today. But if the original prototype had been backed earlier and developed better it could and perhaps should have stolen a march on the Japanese and if it had, the British motorcycle industry in the '70s might have been a different story, too. ■

LEFT: A final version, the T160, displayed what the Trident always should have been, with new styling, improved brakes and even an electric starter.
PHIL WEST

BELOW: Although never the success hoped for, the Trident did have notable success on track, primarily as being the basis for the TT-winning 'Slippery Sam'. PHIL WEST

1969 HONDA CB750

The world's first mass production '750 four' – the superbike was born

The modern era of motorcycling really began with Honda's CB750. As the first mass-produced machine with a 750cc four-cylinder engine it became known as the first 'Superbike' and its success and popularity fuelled the trend for large-capacity, transversely mounted, multi-cylinder engine configurations. In fact, so many other Japanese bikes took their lead from the CB750, such as Kawasaki's Z1 900 and Suzuki's GS1000E, that the CB750 became known as the 'original UJM' – the Universal Japanese Motorcycle.

Along with other technological motorcycling 'firsts', such as its five-speed gearbox, disc front brake and even the electric starter, the CB750's greatest weapon of all was that it was a mass production machine accessible to the masses, thus spawning a whole new era of Japanese dominance.

The creation of the CB is well reported yet is also still often the source of some debate. Although by 1966 Honda was already the world's largest motorcycle manufacturer in terms of volume, the biggest capacity bike it made was still only 450cc – that bike was the famed CB450 Black Bomber twin as launched in 1965.

This machine had been designed specifically to appeal to the huge US market and yet, despite having performance that matched or bettered many larger rivals, Americans still preferred big-cubed Harley-Davidsons and, particularly, British parallel twins such as the Triumph Bonneville. Part of this was down to simply wanting the responsive torque associated with bigger engines so that they could get the power they needed without downshifting. For many riders, motorcycles represented a means of recreation and relaxation rather than rocket-sled performance.

At the same time, in early 1967, after five consecutive GP world titles with its multi-cylinder 350s, sweeping

SPECIFICATIONS

Price new	£680
Engine	736cc air-cooled in-line SOHC four
Power	67bhp @ 8000rpm
Torque	44lb-ft @ 7000rpm
Frame	Tubular steel double cradle
Suspension	35mm telescopic forks (F), twin shocks (R)
Brakes	296mm disc (F), 180mm drum (R)
Tyres	3.25 x 19 (F), 4.00 x 18 (R)
Dry weight	218kg
Top speed	124mph

BELOW: Honda's original superbike, the 1969 CB750K0, especially in initial 'sand cast' form, is now considered one of the most collectable Japanese bikes of all. HONDA

CB-750 K1 Available in Candy Red or Gold and Metallic Green or Brown.

ABOVE: Never really intended as an all-out sports machine (unlike later rivals) the CB750's power of 67bhp was instead targeted to beat Harley's then 1200 tourer. HONDA

RIGHT: The four-into-four exhausts were chosen to emphasise its four-cylinder engine layout. The front disc brake was the first on a mass production machine. HONDA

RIGHT: With targets of being comfortable, smooth, well-equipped and good value, the CB750 proved the final nail in the coffin for the struggling British industry. HONDA

the 250 crown with its RC166 250-6 and winning all five constructors' awards, Honda had made the shock announcement that it would withdraw from GP racing after the FIM (Fédération Internationale de Motocyclisme) announced new regulations restricting 500cc machines to four cylinders and 250 and 350s to twins. Instead, Honda decided it would focus on using that multi-cylinder technology to produce road bikes.

The main target for these new machines was of course the US where, in 1966, Honda sales had actually begun to drop and where customers, according to its US distributors, were crying out for new, big bore machines.

The leader of the project was Yoshiro Harada, who had also developed the Black Bomber. He visited the US in the summer of 1967 to investigate the CB450's impact and even went so far as to detail the bike's superior performance to the staff at American Honda, telling them it was even better than the Nortons and Triumphs. In response, they said that they didn't see the point of a 450 and instead simply took the view that 'bigger was better'. But how big? Honda itself claims the answer came from no less than company founder Soichiro Honda when he visited Switzerland in June 1968.

"A policeman on a white police motorcycle came into the park where we were," the great man is reported as saying. "He then got off his bike. I was watching it, thinking what a small motorcycle he was riding.

"I was amazed to find it was a Triumph 750cc. So, actually the motorcycle was fairly big, but it looked small since the policeman was so big. I knew then that our bikes wouldn't sell in foreign markets if we kept building them according to our Japanese perceptions."

Meanwhile, over at American Honda, service manager Bob Hansen, who that year had flown to Japan and met with Mr Honda to discuss the project, is credited with coming up with the multi-cylinder 750 concept. Over lunch, Honda-san told Hansen they were working on a top secret 'king of motorcycles' idea. Hansen, who knew that Honda already had a 600cc twin cylinder car engine and that Triumph was currently developing a 750 triple that would become the Trident, is reported to have responded that the new bike "better not be a twin", suggesting instead "it should be a four".

Either way, by October 1967, the basics of Honda's new big bike in being a 750 with a peak power output of at least 67bhp (or 1bhp more than Harley's then 1300 big twin) were agreed and, in February 1968, a development team of around 20 was assembled.

With the main aim being superior performance and reliability to rivals from Triumph, BMW and Harley, that 'four-cylinder, four-exhaust' layout was underlined as it was thought that the bike would immediately be associated with Honda's multi-cylinder Grand Prix machines. ▶

LEFT: As well as a glistening gold colour option, Honda's new flagship was initially also offered in blue, red and green options, with the latter currently the rarest. HONDA

Amazingly, just six months later, Harada's team had produced a prototype four-cylinder motor that was a quantum leap over production engines of before.

Horizontally split crankcases minimised the likelihood of oil leaks (a perennial problem associated with British bikes, with their usually vertically split crankcases, up to that time). Its hefty, forged crank complete with plain main bearings, pressure-fed with lubricant, promised longevity and durability. While both the primary drive and the drive for its single overhead camshaft was via chains driven off sprockets in the centre of the crank. There were also two valves per cylinder, a reliable electric starter, indicators that worked flawlessly and that gorgeous four-into-four exhaust. When tested in a CB450 chassis, it immediately proved smooth and fast, so much so that it brought a headache of its own…

With the planned unveiling at the 1968 Tokyo Show fast approaching, one of Harada's big decisions was how to slow the new 750/4 down. Although the test mule used the then usual drum front brake, Harada felt one of the new disc brakes, which by then had started to become popular in racing, was a better choice.

Unable to make up his mind, he approached Soichiro Honda directly. "We've designed two braking systems," he told Mr Honda. "One uses conventional drum brakes and the other disc brakes. Of the two, the disc-brake specification has only recently been developed, so will need more tests. If disc brakes are adopted, we aren't sure we can meet next spring's target."

Honda-san's reply was simple and direct: "Well, of course we'll have to go with disc brakes."

Duly, on October 28, 1968, at the Tokyo Show in Japan, the centrepiece of the Honda stand was the stunning new CB750 rotating silently on a floodlit plinth with an engine mounted on a stand alongside. Never mind that this was a pre-production machine and not the finished article, the motorcycling world was simply stunned.

That Tokyo unveiling also affected motorcycling in less obvious ways. Kawasaki, for example, halted its own secret superbike project, also for a 750 four, but immediately went back to the drawing board only to return a few years later with the 903cc DOHC Z1.

And that, of course, was just the start. With the American market key,

BELOW: The new CB750 also was significantly better equipped than most European rivals of the time, with not only a disc brake but an electric starter as well. HONDA

just as important was Honda's first US dealer meeting held in Las Vegas the following January where the new CB750 was top of the agenda. Four prototypes, in red, blue, green and gold, were displayed.

According to reports, American Honda President, Kihachiro Kawashima, initially announced a price of just $1,295, which caused a furore as that was over a thousand dollars less than any rival and created a clamour for orders – so much so, that Kawashima promptly raised the price to $1,495.

"Since large bikes were selling for between $2,800 and $4,000, all 2,000 dealers burst into thunderous applause when they heard its price," remembered Harada.

Overwhelmed, Honda quickly upscaled production. An initial estimate of 1,500 machines a year had led to early engines being produced by what's referred to as a 'sand-cast' technique to avoid expensive outlay on die-cast tooling for a model they didn't yet know would be profitable. The first production machine duly rolled off the assembly line on March 15, 1969.

British bikers meanwhile, got their first look at the machine that would change motorcycling forever soon after. On April 5, 1969, at the Metropole Hotel, Brighton, venue for the Brighton Motorcycle show, two of the pre-production examples of the all-new Honda CB750, in

ENGINE	
Type	OHC four cylinder, transverse in-line 4-stroke, aluminium alloy, air cooled
Cylinder capacity	736 cc (44·9 cu in)
Bore × stroke	61 × 63 mm (2·4 × 2·48 in)
Compression ratio	9 :1
Carburettors	Four 1·1 in (28 mm) Venturi, piston valve, double float, PW 28
Starting	Electric and kick
Ignition	Coil – battery 12 v 14 ah
Lubrication	Dry sump, separate oil tank
Spark plugs	NGK D-8ES
Clutch	Wet 7 friction disc 5·5 in (140 mm), left hand lever
Transmission	5-speed, constant mesh, left foot pedal return change
Gear ratios	1st 2·500, 2nd 1·708, 3rd 1·333, 4th 1·097, 5th 0·039

PERFORMANCE	
Horsepower	67 bhp/8,000 rpm
Torque	6·1 kg/m (44 ft lb)/7,000 rpm
Braking distance	36 ft (11 m) at 31 mph (50km/h)
Turning circle	16·4 ft (5 m)

FRAME		
Type		Tubular double cradle
Fuel tank capacity		3·9 gal (4·7 US gal, 18 lit) including reserve
Reserve capacity		1·1 gal (1·3 US gal, 5 lit)
Oil system capacity		6 pts (0·93 US gal, 3·5 lit)
Tyres :	Front	3·25 — 19. Air pressure 28 lb/sq in (2 kg/sq cm)
	Rear	4·00 — 18. Air pressure 30 lb/sq in (2·1 kg/sq cm)
Brakes :	Front	Hydraulic disc, 11·7 in (296 mm), right hand lever
	Rear	7 in (180 mm) full width hub, right foot pedal operation
Suspension :	Front	Hydraulic damped telescopic fork, oil capacity 220/230 cc
	Rear	Swinging arm

DIMENSIONS	
Overall length	85 in (2,160 mm)
Overall width	35 in (855 mm)
Overall height	44 in (1,120 mm)
Wheelbase	57·3 in (1,455 mm)
Ground clearance	6·3 in (160 mm)
Seat height	31 in (800 mm)
Footrest height	12 in (310 mm)
Kerb weight (full tank)	481 lb (218 kg)

gold and green, as revealed to US dealers the previous year, were displayed for the very first time, again causing a sensation.

The first press reports were equally enthusiastic, none more so than the leading US magazine, *Cycle World* which, in its August issue, proclaimed: "Some will say it is too heavy or that four cylinders is too many for a motorcycle. But the total is greater than the sum of its parts. If the Four didn't run faster than 120mph, if it didn't turn a 100mph standing quarter mile, it would still be the finest."

Meanwhile, Mick Woollett of the *Motor Cycle*, was the first British journalist to test the CB750 in April of that year. He wrote: "Delightfully smooth and comfortable... a two-wheeled status symbol..."

The flood of orders that ensued from all of this led to that initial 1,500 per year figure quickly being revised to 1,500 and then 3,000 a month. In Britain, the first batch of 25 bikes sold out before they'd even arrived. (As a consequence, those sand-cast examples, identifiable mostly by a rougher finish on the cases and a clutch cover held on by ten rather than 11 screws, are now among the most prized CB750s of all.)

The new CB750 went on to success on track, too, too. Racing versions were developed by Honda's in-house team to compete in the Suzuka Endurance Race in August

ABOVE: Honda's new superbike proved such a sales success it remained largely unchanged for years to come, and stayed in production for nearly a decade. HONDA

BELOW: Today, early (K0 and K1) examples of the CB750 are prized modern classics with one of the original prototypes selling for well over £100,000. HONDA

1969, and dominated with a one-two finish by Blue Helmet MSC. The team of Morio Sumiya and Tetsuya Hishiki took first, while the pairing of Yoichi Oguma and Minoru Sato came a close second. The victory of veteran rider Dick Mann in the Daytona 200 in March 1970 on his CR750 racer sent Stateside customers running to Honda dealers.

In truth and with the benefit of hindsight, the CB750 was more tourer than sportster, revered mostly for its smooth torque than for its outrageous power. But the world's first mass-production four-cylinder motorcycle is today lauded as the first 'superbike' so it is impossible to ignore here.

Just as significant, however, was how successful it was in terms of sales. In the UK, the CB's success effectively killed off any last hopes that the Triumph Trident and BSA Rocket 3 might revive the British industry and, as such, it was instrumental in the collapse of Triumph, BSA, and more in the early 1970s.

The CB's success also helped establish the transverse-four as the new superbike template, spawning a family of Honda spin-offs (including the CB550, CB500 and CB400), not to mention rivals from Kawasaki and Suzuki, while CB750 itself survived in production for almost a decade right up to 1978, by which time nearly half a million had been sold.

That gold prototype, as shown at Brighton, has also proved very significant. While the green bike went on to shows in Europe, the gold one was used for the first road tests (including Woolett's), later sold to the Earl of Denbigh and ultimately became known as 'the Brighton bike'. It was sold at auction at the National Motorcycle Museum in 2018 for a whopping £161,000, making it the most valuable Japanese production bike ever. ■

1971 KAWASAKI 750 MACH IV

The wild 'widowmaker' triple that was the ultimate two-stroke superbike

Motorcycles simply don't get more outrageous or more '1970s' than Kawasaki's hooligan, ballistic, polluting H2 750 Mach IV. The two-stroke triple epitomised the era's lust for performance and glam rock metalflake and chrome, then just as quickly, was killed off after just four years due to the mid-'70s fuel crisis, tightening US emissions regulations and prompting the rise of Kawasaki's own Z1 superbike.

The Japanese brand had already stunned the motorcycling world with its 500cc H1 Mach III in 1969, a riotous two-stroke triple producing 60bhp. For 1972, therefore, inspired by both Honda's CB750 and the newly formed Formula 750 production-based race series, a 750cc Mach IV was almost inevitable.

Despite being inspired by the 500, the 750 was much more than just an enlarged version of it. A new model from the ground up, it used easier-to-balance triangular flywheels, its main bearings were larger, and its port timing milder. Its chassis was a big improvement, too, with a stiffer frame, improved braking via a front disc in place of the 500's drum and the result, the 748cc H2 Mach IV unveiled in late 1971, produced 74bhp, the most powerful of the

SPECIFICATIONS	
Price new	£758
Engine	748cc air-cooled two-stroke triple
Power	74bhp @ 6,800rpm
Torque	57lb-ft @ 6,500rpm
Frame	Tubular steel double cradle
Suspension	36mm telescopic forks (F), twin shocks (R)
Brakes	295mm disc (F), 200mm drum (R)
Tyres	3.25 x 19 (F), 4.00 x 18 (R)
Dry weight	192kg
Top speed	126mph

day – six more than the CB and seven more than Suzuki's GT.

Kawasaki weren't modest about their new beast, either. "We've just pulled a fast one on the competition," said early adverts. "Of all the world's production models, it's the fastest thing on two wheels. Faster than any Suzuki. Faster than any Triumph. Faster than any BSA, and Honda, any anything."

Magazine tests were equally euphoric. "The new 750 Mach IV

is a rocket," wrote the US's *Cycle*. "The Mach IV is worth every extra nickel for the sheer pleasure of leaping from a dead stop to 100mph in less time than it takes the average rider to buckle his helmet."

Trouble was, that wasn't the whole story. That two-stroke power rush came all at once and the spindly, lightweight chassis could barely cope. The H2 flexed in corners, weaved down straights, and was so wheelie prone it soon earned the nickname 'Widowmaker'.

A racing version, the H2R, also debuted in 1972, and in its striking 'Green Meanie' livery in the hands of the likes of Yvon Duhamel, Gary Nixon in the US, and Mick Grant and Barry Ditchburn in the UK, became a fixture of early 1970s racing.

With the benefit of hindsight, it probably couldn't last – and it didn't. By 1973, with the arrival of Kawasaki's new flagship Z1 900, plus the oil crisis which prompted increasingly strict environmental and emissions regulations, it was obvious that the 22mpg H2's days were numbered.

After the first H1 came the updated 1973 H1A then restyled, revised, longer wheelbase H2B in 1974 before the final 'C' of 1975, by which time an estimated 47,000 of all types had been built. Today, however, the brilliant but bonkers H2, is among the most collectable of all Kawasakis, with auction prices regularly above £20K. ■

ABOVE: The 750 H2 Mach VI was the biggest and wildest of Kawasaki's series of 1960s and 1970s two-stroke triples which also included a 250, 350, 400 and 500. KAWASAKI

LEFT: The original was the 1969 500 H1 Mach III, on which the Mach IV was derived. Note the old-style drum front brake. KAWASAKI

1971 SUZUKI GT750

The water cooled, two-stroke triple that became known as 'The Kettle'

While Honda was the first manufacturer to produce a new breed of 750cc, multi-cylinder superbike with its four-stroke CB750, two of its Japanese rivals quickly responded with two-stroke machines: Kawasaki with its H2 750 Mach IV and Suzuki with its GT750.

Yet although both were 750cc 'stroker' triples, to ride they could not have been much more different. The Kawasaki was the wild, loud hooligan, the Suzuki the far more genteel and leisurely grand tourer.

The GT750 came first and was unveiled at the Tokyo Show at the end of 1970. At 738cc, its all new three-cylinder engine was the largest two-stroke yet produced, while it also pioneered water cooling, which led to its nickname 'the kettle'.

However, although targeted at Honda's 68bhp CB, the 67bhp GT was also far heavier due to its water cooling and radiator, and was slightly bulky and cumbersome as a result, and so never quite snatched the Honda's performance crown.

Even so, the Suzuki was still a success – and far more so than Kawasaki's more dramatic and dynamic but short-lived H2. Where the H2 was wild, raw, lairy and intimidating, the GT was smooth, 'grunty', luxurious and cossetting with its 115mph and 40mpg more than enough for most.

The GT was also equipped with an electric starter and twin discs as early as a 1973 makeover, popular both with tech buffs due to its pioneering liquid-cooling and two-stroke fans, and ultimately proved an enduring success that lived on as Suzuki's flagship right up to 1978 (when it was succeeded by the four-stroke GS750) with a total of 71,000 sold worldwide.

The GT had more than a little success in sport, too. A racing version, the TR750, debuted in 1972, and, despite notoriously wayward handling, this 120bhp version was one of the fastest racers of the early 1970s, propelling new Suzuki star Barry Sheene to the 1973 F750 title before being replaced by Suzuki's revolutionary square four RG500 grand prix machine in 1975. Less gloriously, however, the TR was also the bike Sheene was riding in his infamous 175mph Daytona 200 crash earlier that same year. ■

BELOW: The radiator and water-cooling system made the GT heavy, but it was still a decent performer and pioneered twin disc front brakes. SUZUKI

Suzuki's entry into the new 750 superbike class was also a two-stroke triple, the GT750, but was targeted as a tourer and was water cooled. SUZUKI

SPECIFICATIONS

Price new	£766.50
Engine	738cc liquid-cooled two-stroke triple
Power	67bhp @ 6,500rpm
Torque	51lb-ft @ 5,500rpm
Frame	Tubular steel double cradle
Suspension	35mm telescopic forks (F), twin shocks (R)
Brakes	203mm TLS drum (F), 200mm SLS drum (R)
Tyres	3.25 x 19 (F), 4.00 x 18 (R)
Dry weight	214kg
Top speed	115mph

1972 KAWASAKI
Z1 900

The new superbike king that redefined 1970s motorcycle performance

Honda's 1969 CB750 may have been the first 'superbike' but the Z1 which followed from Japanese rivals Kawasaki was every bit as significant.

Designed to leapfrog the CB in every way, the big 'Zed', at a 750-busting 903cc and with twin cams (instead of the CB's one) producing a whopping 82bhp, was bigger, more sophisticated and more powerful than the Honda, and established a new superbike benchmark that would dominate for the rest of the decade. Kawasaki's newcomer did just that and the Z1 was not only the most powerful, fastest superbike around, right up to 1977's Suzuki GS1000, it became the go-to engine for racers, drag strip demons and specials builders, and was voted Machine of the Year by the UK's *Motor Cycle News* (*MCN*) for four years in succession.

The Z1's inspiration came directly from Honda. Kawasaki had coincidentally been developing its own 750 four when the CB750 was unveiled in 1968, forcing it back to the drawing board with a vow to respond with something

SPECIFICATIONS

Price new	£1,177
Engine	903cc air-cooled in-line DOHC four
Power	82bhp @ 8,500rpm
Torque	54lb-ft @ 7,000rpm
Frame	Tubular steel double cradle
Suspension	36mm telescopic forks (F), twin shocks (R)
Brakes	296mm disc (F), 200mm drum (R)
Tyres	3.50 x 19 (F), 4.00 x 18 (R)
Dry weight	230kg
Top speed	134mph

ABOVE: The Z1 also featured bolder, more aggressive styling than the Honda CB750 – most notably with its distinctive 'duck bill' rear seat unit. KAWASAKI

LEFT: The 'DOHC' said it all – nearly. Instead of Honda's SOHC 750, the Z1 was a DOHC 900. KAWASAKI

ABOVE: After being forced back to the drawing board with its own 750 due to the unveiling of Honda's CB750, Kawasaki responded with its 900cc Z1. KAWASAKI

even bigger, faster and more sophisticated. The 903cc, double overhead cam (DOHC), 18bhp more powerful Z1 was exactly that, and reigned as performance king for most of the decade, providing the template for most superbike fours which followed.

Kawasaki's own idea for a four-cylinder four-stroke dated back to 1967. Up until then, the Japanese marque had focused mainly on developing two-stroke motorcycles, with the exception of its 1966 W1 650, a British-style four-stroke parallel twin that evolved from a licensed design from BSA, its A7.

But with the success of the Z1 and with a desire to further expand into four-strokes, Kawasaki then decided to develop a high-performance motorcycle which would far exceed the 650W1 with the goal being a fast yet comfortable 750 with good handling and brakes – a modern version, it claimed later, of the 1950s' Vincent HRD Black Shadow.

Duly, at Kawasaki's head office at Akashi in Japan in 1967, company bosses instructed a team of its best engineers led by Gyoichi 'Ben' Inamura and co-ordinated by Sam Tanegashima, to develop a programme centred around a large capacity, four-cylinder four-stroke motorcycle with an engine size of 750cc. Kawasaki was primarily looking east, noting a rise in desire among American riders for ever bigger motors with increasing touring speeds, and knew it had to be first of the Japanese marques to bring such a machine to market. A planning group was quickly established under the internal development code T103 and the project was codenamed 'New York Steak'. Why? Because the Japanese considered the best meal in America to be NY steak and the Z1 was also conceived to be the very best, at the top of the menu.

The resulting 750cc four-cylinder mock-up was completed in October 1968 but, unfortunately for Kawasaki, at the very same time, Honda unveiled its all-new, production ready, 750cc single overhead cam (SOHC) CB750 four at the Tokyo Motor Show.

Stunned, Kawasaki management immediately realised it was meaningless to come out with a similar model after Honda had already introduced theirs, so all development efforts on Kawasaki's 750 was stopped. Fortunately for us – and superbike development history – that wasn't the end. Kawasaki became determined to 'out-do' the CB and, in 1970, the Z1 developing project team was reunited with the best staff in all fields joining the project. This group repeated research and experiments to develop an even better bike. Kawasaki resumed US market research in March 1970 by collecting customer opinions from various sources such as random samplings of dealers and editors of major motorcycle magazines, and, finally, Kawasaki management concluded there was a strong market for a

LEFT: The reaction to the Z1's launch was so positive that Kawasaki initially struggled to keep up with demand. KAWASAKI

high-speed motorcycle with visual appeal, and enough power to use as a reliable touring model.

This time Kawasaki's four cylinder was conceived to be 'The king of motorcycles' and to not just beat the Honda – but decimate it. So, despite a 'gentleman's agreement' between the Japanese manufacturers to keep their machines under 750cc, Kawasaki decided to enlarge its four, take its capacity as big as deemed possible within the existing casings, which resulted in an 'oversquare' 66 x 66mm bore and stroke (compared to the traditional long stroke Honda) taking capacity up to a whopping 903cc, making it not only the largest motorcycle in Japan but, worldwide; larger than the Italian Moto Guzzi 850 and comparable even to the Harley-Davidson 1000 and 1200. The new Kawasaki also featured twin camshafts, more sophisticated bucket and shim adjusters, and a five-speed gearbox (the Honda had a four speeder). Similarly, its pressed-up crank with its roller bearings, owed more to Kawasaki's own two-stroke design background than to the CB750's car-style plain bearing crank.

Double overhead cams (DOHC) were necessary to realise overall high performance from low to high-speed rpms. In motorcycle markets around the world, there were only one or two other samples of this type of engine, and the Z1

was the first Kawasaki to adopt this advanced valve train system.

Otherwise, the main features of the Z1 were a traditional tubular steel double cradle frame with telescopic forks and twin shock rear, the new safe and reliable disc brake system, and, just as importantly, ease of maintenance. Since the Z1 utilised the complicated DOHC mechanism, ease of maintenance was carefully considered at the design stage. As a result, the Z1 could be maintained without removing the engine from the motorcycle, except for maintenance of crankshaft-related parts.

Styling was also important. The Z1 was intended to be fresh, but 'cool', without the look of a 900cc heavyweight machine. This was achieved with 'tail-up' silencers, a light-looking 'teardrop' fuel tank, and a slim, flowing seat, with all parts individually examined and tested time after time.

In total, the project would take three years. The first prototype was completed in the spring of 1971. This was then ridden by American test riders (as the US was its primary intended market), sometimes even with Honda tank badges, with minor adjustments made step by step. *Cycle* magazine journalist Bryon Farnsworth had been the first, flying to Japan in 1971 and subsequently taking on the role of senior US tester for the new machine. In the autumn

> ## " *Kawasaki's four-cylinder was conceived to be 'The King of Motorcycles'* "

ABOVE: Not just larger in capacity, the new Z1 was more powerful than the Honda, more imposing, and faster too – a new king of superbikes. KAWASAKI

BELOW: Updates were minor in the early years. First year bikes had black engines then, later, the bike was renamed as the Z900 with a 1000 eventually following. KAWASAKI

of that year, the final prototype was completed and after further testing, during which all parts, including even the nuts and bolts, were examined, the bike was approved for mass production. After reworking any weak points, the first mass-production model was built in May then further tested for durability and reliability. Later that year Kawasaki rented Talladega Speedway in Alabama for a full 30-day stint and its testing team, including racers American Gary Nixon and Brit Paul Smart, ran test mules mercilessly flat out for entire tankful's of fuel. Nothing was left to chance.

In September 1972, the Z1 was introduced to the US public, then revealed to a stunned European motorcycle audience at the 1972 IFMA motorcycle show in Cologne, with sales starting in November that year.

Everyone who sampled the Z1 was simply blown away by its numbers. Its maximum horsepower was 82hp at 8,500rpm – a full 13 more than Honda's CB750 and 8hp more than Kawasaki's own two-stroke H2. Interestingly, however, the Z1's horsepower per displacement figure was lower than that of the H1 and H2 as Kawasaki had changed its engine design policy so that its powerband was no longer set near the engine's limit, thereby pursuing smoother, more flexible engine performance. It is also noteworthy that the Z1 engine was based on a policy to prevent pollution and was equipped

with anti-air-pollution devices such as a positive crankcase ventilation system. Clearly, therefore, the Z1 also had great tuning potential (especially considering the average horsepower of a 1200cc car at that time was 77hp).

The Z1 could also accelerate from zero to 400m in just 12 seconds and its top speed was over 130mph.

While soon after its launch, Kawasaki ramped up publicity further by taking its new baby (and factory riders Duhamel, Art Baumann and Gary Nixon) to Daytona after that year's 200 race, where over two days it set a new world speed record by averaging 109.6mph for 24 hours.

"Kawasaki has made the first step into the realm of the New Superbikes," wrote leading US magazine *Cycle News* in one of the first magazine tests. "The Z1 is fast, luxurious, reliable, pleasant to ride and can even be fun. Kawasaki is waiting, World."

Cycle magazine, meanwhile, added: "Horsepower flows… like water from an artesian well. It simply never stops."

Accordingly, the bike nicknamed 'The New York Steak', was enthusiastically welcomed by markets as the 'mouth-watering motorcycle' when sales started, with over 1,500 examples being sold a month, including the European markets, in its first months.

German enthusiast Franz Volkman of Speyer was one of an elite group of purchasers who bought the brand-new bike when it became available.

"I first saw the 900 Z1 at the IFMA motorcycle show in Cologne in September 1972 and instantly wanted it and ordered one right away," he recalled years later. "It was one of the first delivered in March 1973 and I asked my Kawasaki dealer to give me a ring when the crate was delivered. He rang me at work when it arrived, and I took the rest of the day off!

"What was so amazing about the Z1? Besides its great design, it was all about power. The powerful engine with a claimed 82 horsepower made it the strongest bike in the market. Nothing came close to the Z1. Everything on the Z1 felt right, as if each and every part was designed and crafted by engineers."

It was all enough for the Kawasaki Z1 to become an instant sensation

ABOVE: Final incarnations at the end of the 1970s included a restyled, angular Z1000 and, only for the American market, even a limited edition turbo! KAWASAKI

BELOW: As well as the (very 1970s) brown and orange colour scheme, the Z1 was also offered in a metallic green and yellow option. KAWASAKI

and immediately establish itself as the new performance king. At 903cc, with twin cams producing a whopping 82bhp, the 'Zed' was bigger, more sophisticated and more powerful than the CB750, establishing a new superbike benchmark. The Z1 was also loved not just by '70s riders wanting the ultimate street bike but also drag racers, specials builders, and more. Reputedly inspiring Suzuki's own GS750/1000, it remained in production until being updated by the 1975 Z900 by which time an estimated 85,000 had been built. It was also voted 'Machine of the Year' by readers of the UK's *Motor Cycle News,* not just once but for four years in succession.

Today the 903cc Z1 has become a motorcycling icon, revered as the first motorcycle in a history of Z models, and, for many enthusiasts and industry experts, by combining advanced technical features and what has become recognised as a timeless design, the Z1 is one of the most coveted collector's machines in the world of motorcycling and a machine of great historical significance.

Inspirational and innovative, the four-cylinder, across the four led to an array of further successful Z machines, starting with the 1976 Z650, and acted as technical and design inspiration for many subsequent Kawasaki models in the Z line, including the current Z750, streetfighter style Z1000, its pioneering 1990s retros, the Zephyr family, Kawasaki's whole modern day 'Z' family of roadsters, and even its latest generation of retros, the Z650RS and Z900RS.

King of Motorcycles? Not half… ■

The 1973 750 SuperSport was Ducati's very first 90° V-twin (or 'L-twin' as Ducati calls it) superbike with desmodromic valves. DUCATI

1973 DUCATI 750 SUPERSPORT

The first Desmo V-twin which set the template for all Ducatis that followed

Simply, the 1973 Ducati 750 SuperSport is one of the most significant Italian superbikes of all time. Effectively a road, production replica of the Desmo V-twin racer that British star Paul Smart famously rode to victory at the inaugural Imola 200 in April 1972, it was Ducati's first production 'L-twin' with desmodromic valves (the preceding 750 GT and 750 Sport were both bevel-drive driven), while its fine handling chassis, disc brakes and replica bodywork, including fairing in silver/green, established the very idea of racer-replica Ducati sports exotica. To put it another way: without the 750 SuperSport, the whole Ducati V-twin superbike 'thing' might never have happened… no 851, no 916, no King Carl Fogarty, no Desmosedici and no Panigale… No wonder then that

today, the 750 SuperSport is one of the most collectable (and valuable) Ducatis of all.

The 750 SuperSport's 'back story' is synonymous and inseparable from one man – legendary Ducati designer 'Ing' Fabio Taglioni. Although experimenting with desmodromic valve actuation as early as the 1950s, in the early 1960s he was more significant for a more conventional machine. Ducati's US importer had asked the factory for a bike targeted at the US. Taglioni came up with the first Scrambler, a bevel drive, 250cc trail-style single-cylinder four-stroke which was a big hit Stateside, put Ducati well and truly on the map, and spawned a whole family of street scrambler singles from 125 to 350cc.

But by the late 1960s Ducati's fortunes had nose-dived. A new

wave of ever larger, more powerful, multi-cylinder Japanese machines headlined by Honda's CB750 had risen to dominance, Ducati had been absorbed, in 1969, into a state-run entity, and Taglioni was then tasked by its new management to both build a 750 superbike with which to compete (but using, for cost reasons, as much technology

BELOW:
Desmodromic valve operation had been the brainchild of Ducati chief engineer 'Ing' Fabio Taglioni, who first trialed the system on smaller machines. DUCATI

SPECIFICATIONS

Price new	$3,200
Engine	748cc air-cooled 90° desmodromic V-twin
Power	72bhp @ 9,000rpm
Torque	52.8lb-ft @ 5,500rpm
Frame	Tubular steel double cradle
Suspension	38mm telescopic forks (F), twin shocks (R)
Brakes	2 x 275mm disc (F), 230mm disc (R)
Tyres	3.50 x 18 (F), 4.00 x 18 (R)
Dry weight	151kg
Top speed	130mph

from its existing singles as possible), and to initiate a return to racing to promote them, first in 500GPs.

In February 1970, Taglioni showed bosses the first drawing of his proposed solution: a 90° 750cc V-twin that was essentially two bevel-drive singles grafted together which allowed the use of as many Scrambler parts as possible, gave ideal primary balance (due to the 90° arrangement) while its longitudinal layout meant the engine was narrow, so could be carried low in the frame while also maintaining good ground clearance. Given the green light, that first bevel drive engine initially powered the 750 GT, launched in 1971, so becoming the first production V-twin in Ducati history.

At the same time, alongside the 750, Taglioni was also working on a desmodromic 500cc GP V-twin which was first campaigned in late 1970. But, with power down compared to MV Agusta's dominant triples, success was slow.

That all changed in 1971 with the announcement of the first Imola 200 race which had been conceived as a big purse 'European Daytona 200' open to 750cc machines which was to take place on April 23, 1972, and attracted entrants from all the leading manufacturers. Ducati instructed Taglioni to mount a full-scale assault, seven race 750 'desmos' based on both the 750GT and 500GP bikes were built in record time and Paul Smart was hired at the last minute before going on to win a legendary Ducati 1-2 ahead of regular factory rider Bruno Spaggiari.

The result not only put Ducati on the superbike map, but it also established the firm's signature for sporting desmo L-twins. As Taglioni himself said in 1974: "When we won at Imola, we won the market, too."

A road-going replica, the 750 Supersport, came first at the end of 1973, immediately proved a sensation and spawned a whole family of spin-offs. Later, in 1978, with both 750 and 900cc production L-twins established, Mike Hailwood came out of retirement to win a fairytale F1 TT aboard a 900cc NCR-prepared version, and Ducati's superbike 'signature' was well and truly set.

The real significance of the Super Sport, of course, was not that it was a 'first', but that it worked so well. Based on the already impressive 748cc, 90° V-twin from the 750GT, but with the desmodromic valves of the racer, it also had a raised compression ratio of 10.5:1 (up from 8.5:1), and bigger 40mm carbs which together helped boost power significantly to 72bhp, up from the GT's 50.

That performance, combined with a claimed light dry weight of just

ABOVE: The Briton had been drafted into the factory team at the last moment to support lead rider Bruno Spaggiari and ended up winning. DUCATI

BELOW: It was created as a limited-edition road-going replica of the racing machine Paul Smart famously rode to victory in the 1972 Imola 200. DUCATI

151kg (Kawasaki's then superbike king Z1 may have produced 84bhp but it also weighed a hefty 230kg dry), plus a fine-handling chassis with the very best suspension and brakes from the likes of Marzocchi and Brembo, added up to the best performing 750 of the day. While, with a sporty riding position, racy fairing and Imola replica green/silver paint job, Ducati's new 750 was also one of the best-looking motorcycles around. It wasn't cheap, of course, but it was certainly some kind of ultimate superbike.

Unfortunately for Ducati, however, the 750 Super Sport, although undoubtedly a success, was also not the money-maker it could and maybe should have been. Designer Taglioni's glorious 'round case' Desmo V-twin engine proved difficult and expensive to make, causing production delays with the result that only 401 examples were built in 1974.

To improve things, Taglioni was asked to design a simpler, cheaper bevel drive system and Giorgetto Giugiaro of Ital Design came up with a new 'square case' engine case design which, together with an enlarged 864cc capacity, resulted in the 900 Super Sport of 1975. But although competent, successful and prized, things were never quite the same.

But those original, rare, exquisite and short-lived 'round-case' 750s have become some of the most collectible motorcycles of all. ∎

1973 BENELLI SEI 750

The outrageous six-cylinder which beat Honda's CBX by five years

RIGHT: After de Tomaso bought Benelli in 1971, the company was relaunched with a bold new flagship – the six cylinder 750cc Sei. BENELLI

BELOW: Although striking and pioneering, the Sei was also blighted by production difficulties and a high price, and was never the success hoped for. BENELLI

Few superbikes of the early to mid-1970s were as exotic, expensive, outrageous – or, tragically, as flawed – as Italian marque Benelli's short-lived 750 'Sei'.

The 'Sei' (Italian for 'six) was the world's first production six-cylinder motorcycle a full six years before Honda's equally outlandish CBX1000, yet it also boasted gorgeous Italian styling, complete with a six-outlet exhaust and top-quality Italian cycle parts such as Marzocchi suspension, Brembo brakes, and alloy-rimmed Borrani wire wheels.

As such, on paper at least, the Sei effectively married the high-tech, multi-cylinder technology and performance of the Japanese with the exotic style and specification of European machines and thus could – and perhaps, *should* – have been the most powerful, fastest, best handling and desirable motorcycle of the 1970s. Instead, production delays, underwhelming performance, iffy reliability and build quality, and a price more than double that of Kawasaki's new Z1 superbike king, consigned the Sei to be one of superbiking's great failures.

The Sei was the pet project of ambitious Argentine entrepreneur Alejandro de Tomaso who originally rose to prominence by founding the De Tomaso sports car company in Italy, later most famous for the Ford V8-engined Pantera. In 1971, he also took over ailing Italian bike legend Benelli and promptly directed its engineers to come up with a new six-cylinder flagship with beautiful Italian styling and the best of components. When he unveiled the first prototype just over a year later, de Tomaso famously stated that he was "declaring war on the Japanese motorcycle".

That rushed, short development period hinted at why the Sei never quite delivered on that promise. For expediency's sake, the engine was effectively that of Honda's SOHC CB500/4 but with two extra cylinders, it proved unreliable and produced only 71bhp (when Kawasaki's Z1 already had 82). Although beautiful and desirable (it was styled by Ghia, which de Tomaso also owned), production problems caused delays and quality issues. And although a fine handler with top quality cycle parts, it was also prohibitively expensive and proved a sales flop, with just 293 built in 1974 and only a further 3,000 or so up to 1977.

Refusing to admit defeat, de Tomaso updated the 750 and released the enlarged, restyled Sei 900 in 1973 – but it was all too little, too late. By then Honda's own more sophisticated twin overhead cam far more powerful 105bhp six, the CBX1000, was available, and the Sei failed again with just under 2,000 produced.

Today, however, the Sei, in both its guises, remains one of the most astounding and collectable 1970s Italian classics of all. ■

SPECIFICATIONS

Price new	$3,995 (in the US)
Engine	748cc air-cooled in-line SOHC six
Power	71bhp @ 8,500rpm
Torque	61lb-ft @ 7,000rpm
Frame	Tubular steel double cradle
Suspension	Telescopic forks (F), twin shocks (R)
Brakes	2 x 300mm discs (F), 200mm drum (R)
Tyres	3.25 x 18 (F), 4.10 x 18 (R)
Dry weight	220kg
Top speed	127mph

1974 JOHN PLAYER NORTON

The British twin that was arguably the very first 'racer replica'

Price new	$2,995 (in the US)
Engine	829cc air cooled pushrod parallel twin
Power	60bhp @ 6,200rpm
Torque	N/a
Frame	Tubular steel double cradle
Suspension	Telescopic forks (F), twin shocks (R)
Brakes	Single disc (F), drum (R)
Tyres	4.10 x 19 (F), 4.10 x 19 (R)
Dry weight	188kg
Top speed	115mph

It's a common motorcycling misconception that the 1985 GSX-R750F was the first 'racer replica', being modelled on Suzuki's 1983 XR41 works endurance racer – it wasn't. Over a decade earlier Italian legends MV produced road-going replicas of its iconic four-cylinder GP racers, albeit at 750 not 500cc, while in 1974 British brand Norton, on face value at least, went further still with its 850 John Player Replica.

The new Formula 750 motorcycle racing class introduced in the early 1970s had a big influence on mainstream motorcycling, spawning many 750cc machines created to race in the series. The production-based series launched in the US in 1971, in world championships in 1972, and in the UK in 1973, prompted not only the creation of the Rob North-framed BSA/Triumph triples which won the 1971 Daytona 200 and spawned the first Anglo-American Match Races soon after, but also prompted Dennis Poore, Norton chairman, to commission a one-off F750 prototype based on the 750 Commando.

The bike was developed by factory racer and development engineer Peter Williams who compensated for the Norton's lack of power with aerodynamics and superior handling and, with sponsorship from John Player tobacco, the first, blue-liveried bikes, ridden mostly by Williams and Phil Read, showed promise.

But in 1973, Williams' all-new monocoque chassis proved a revelation and, with new bodywork in striking white/red and blue, and a rider line-up of Williams and Dave Croxford in matching leathers, the 'JP Nortons' dominated British racing, Williams won three rounds of the Transatlantic Trophy, the F750 TT, and was placed second in the *MCN* superbike championship, with Croxford winning the British 750cc series.

Following that success and with the failing Norton factory desperate for a sales 'winner', it was then decided to build a limited edition, road-going replica. In truth, with limited funds and no monocoque, the result was little more than a lookalike – a standard Mk2A Commando 850 with facsimile bodywork comprised of a one-piece fairing/tank cover made by Avon, plus a matching single seat in replica white/red and blue. The performance from the ageing pushrod twin was unchanged at 60bhp, there was still just a four-speed gearbox and single Lockheed disc brake, tank capacity was miserly, and, for taller riders, it was uncomfortable, too.

But the replica was also arguably the raciest British-built bike yet, looked easily worth its $500 premium over the standard version and, with just 200 made, proved an immediate hit. Sadly, by the time it went on sale, John Player's race sponsorship had ended, the F750 race team had been disbanded, and Norton itself was on its last legs. Today the John Player Replica remains probably the most iconic and collectable British superbike of the 1970s. ■

LEFT: Forget Suzuki's GSX-R750, the John Player Norton was the first 'true' racer replica, even if it was merely a cosmetic restyle of a standard Commando. AUTHOR'S OWN

LEFT: It was inspired by the truly revolutionary Norton monocoque F1 machine which was developed (and ridden) by Peter Williams. AUTHOR'S OWN

1974 HONDA GOLD WING

Four-cylinders, 1,000cc... but not quite the superbike Honda hoped for

Today, the Gold Wing, which celebrated its 50th year in production in 2025, is one of the most successful motorcycle models of all time, with over 100,000 sold. It is now the very definition of a long distance tourer or, in the current guise, a 'full dresser'. So, it may come as some surprise to learn that the 1975 original was launched as a 'naked' superbike and initially had only very limited success.

In 1972, four years after the unveiling of its CB750, which had become known as the first superbike, Honda was facing increasing competition to its supremacy. In 1971 Suzuki and Kawasaki had come up with the GT750 and 750 H2 respectively, then the following year the CB750 had been well and truly overtaken by Kawasaki's Z1 900.

In a bid to regain Honda's mantle of superbike kings, no less than boss Soichiro Honda himself set up a design team led by Shoichiro Irimajiri, who had headed up Honda's five and six-cylinder road racing engines in the 1960s, to explore a concept called 'the king of motorcycles'.

With hindsight, the brief for the prototype that came to be called the 'M1' was slightly muddled. Though aiming to create a new superbike king, Honda was also mindful of the continuing Stateside popularity of traditional tourers from Harley-Davidson, BMW and Moto Guzzi, and wanted to create the largest, fastest and best touring machine ever produced.

The resulting prototype achieved that goal: it was a liquid-cooled flat six displacing a whopping 1470cc (just 2cc shy of double the CB750's). It also boasted shaft drive, a CB750-beating 80bhp, reported top speed of 130mph, and all up weight of 265kg. Unfortunately, however, the sheer length of the engine made a comfortable riding position almost impossible. Honda himself baulked at its massive size and the M1 was canned.

Yet the overall 'king of kings' project, now revised to be an innovative, world beating grand tourer, continued. A new project leader, Toshio Nozue, took over from Irimajiri, as the 1470cc flat six had been deemed too big, a 999cc four-cylinder version was arrived at, and a new name – Gold Wing – after the Honda company logo, emphasised its significance.

Not that this new, smaller version was in any way less innovative. As the flat four layout still required liquid-cooling (primarily to cool the rear cylinders), Nozue's team came up with the world's first liquid-cooled four-stroke motorcycle

ABOVE: The project to create the Gold Wing originally set out to be a superbike under the 'king of kings' tagline in response to Kawasaki's Z1. HONDA

(liquid-cooled two strokes had been done as long ago as 1908 by Scott and, more recently, by Suzuki's GT750 'kettle') by studying car designs from Porsche, BMW, and Chevrolet. Although impressively compact, the new bike's still hefty weight dictated motorcycling's first standard twin disc front brake set-up (a second disc had only been an option on Kawasaki's 1972 H2), while the downdraft carbs and airbox dictated a pioneering 'hidden' under seat fuel tank.

The result, the first GL1000K0 Gold Wing, was unveiled at Honda's US dealer show at Las Vegas in September 1974, then publicly launched in Europe at Cologne the following month and, despite the presence of plenty of other new hardware, including the new CB400F, it stole the show.

Despite impressing in some early tests – US magazine *Cycle* put it through the standing quarter in early 1975 at just 12.92 seconds, slower only than the Z1 and recently deleted H2, with a top speed of over 120mph – public opinion was initially mixed.

Some thought its massive weight of 265kg excessive, resulting in a

ABOVE RIGHT: Instead, when launched, it had been reduced slightly to a 1000cc flat four that was now targeted more at the US touring market. HONDA

RIGHT: The first prototype, dubbed the 'M1', was a flat six but was canned as it made the riding position awkward. HONDA

BELOW: The Gold Wing has since proved to be one of Honda's most successful models, with the latest incarnation back to being a six-cylinder displacing 1800cc. HONDA

'Lead Wing' nickname. Others, most infamously the UK's *Bike* magazine, derided it as a 'Two Wheeled Motor Car?' before describing it as 'ugly, overweight, too complicated and boring', enough for the publication to lose Honda's advertising for a year. While the hefty US price of $2,889 put buyers off, too.

The overall result was that, while Honda had been hoping to recreate the success of its 1969 CB750, when tens of thousands of the new superbike were sold in the first year alone, the new 'Wing, instead of the targeted 60,000 sales in its first 12 months, sold just 5,000. The disappointment was massive.

From there, however, things improved – particularly in the US. In 1976 a new advertising campaign focused on the 'Wing's core merits as a fast grand tourer and over 20,000 were sold. The increasing availability of aftermarket fairings from the likes of Vetter and Rickman further improved its touring credentials, while the evolution of the 'Wing itself saw it gradually establish itself as motorcycling's most luxurious tourer. In 1976 a limited edition was added with more traditional 'cruiser' styling

details, and in 1978 it gained new Comstar wheels, updated styling and improved suspension.

But the biggest changes came after 1980. That year it not only grew to 1100cc, an additional model, the GL1100 Interstate, was announced, this time with full fairing and hard luggage. It was the first mass-produced Japanese motorcycle with full touring kit, a huge sales success, and the 'Wing's status as 'king of tourers' was set in motion.

A third model, the even more luxurious Aspencade, came in 1982, and in 1984 it grew again to 1200cc. At the same time, Honda began work on an all-new, even larger successor that would cement the 'Wing as 'ultimate tourer' once and for all.

The result, the 1988 GL1500 six, did exactly that, seeing off all rivals, surviving in production a full 13 years and becoming the definitive 'full dresser' before that too was replaced by the 2001 GL1800, then all-new version in 2018 which lives on to this day.

Today's Gold Wing may be far removed from its 1975 'superbike' original, but without the GL1000, it might never have existed at all. ■

1976 BMW

The 1970s marked the beginning of a new era for BMW motorcycles. The historic German marque had entered the decade facing an uncertain future, threatened mostly by a new wave of multi-cylinder machines from the Far East. While BMW's 1960 R69S had been a success, subsequent models had seemed increasingly dated and expensive, and by 1969 the company's bikes were viewed by many as both overly conservative and expensive, especially compared to the new wave of Japanese superbikes.

BMW had been inextricably linked to the shaft-drive boxer twin powertrain ever since its first bike, the R32 of 1923, but by the late 1960s it was increasingly seen as hackneyed and underwhelming. It was time for a big boost for the boxer twin, both in terms of performance and style. That duly came in the 1970s, first with the 1973 R90S then, even more so, with its successor, the radical 1976 R100RS.

A significant step forward towards both advances came with the opening of BMW's new Berlin plant, in Spandau, previously used to make car components, in 1969. A new, much improved, range of bikes – the /5 series – then came shortly afterwards but the company still desperately needed a new flagship. To create it, BMW first enlarged 1972's R75/6 to 898cc and 60bhp to result in the biggest, most powerful boxer yet. The 1973 R90/6 then quickly followed that bike up – as it had done with the previous R69 – with a special 'S' version. The resulting 1973 R90S had a higher compression ratio and bigger carbs to boost peak power to 67bhp, a second front disc for improved braking power, while stylist Hans Muth gave it a distinct identity by way of a handlebar fairing (a world first on a production machine) and radical 1970s smoked metalflake colour schemes. Presented on the 50th anniversary of BMW Motorrad in the autumn of 1973, the R90S caused a sensation.

In truth, the result wasn't either as fast and powerful as Kawasaki's Z1 900, as fine handling as a Ducati 750 SuperSport, nor as luxurious as the biggest Harleys. But as a combination of all three, as a 120mph-plus sports-tourer with high-speed cruising ability, comfort, handling and BMW's traditional reliability and quality, the R90S was second to none. It also, to the surprise of some, proved good enough to win on track. Steve McLaughlin celebrated victory on the R90S at the Daytona 200 in the spring of 1976; Hans-Otto Butenuth and Helmut Dahn rode an R90S to a class win in the 1976 Production TT, and it also proved good enough

ABOVE: The fairing itself was styled by then in-house designer Hans Muth and aerodynamically developed at Pininfarina's wind tunnel in Italy. BMW

> **The RS was the ultimate 'gentleman's express'**

R100RS

The faired wonder that put BMW on the superbike map

ABOVE: It was launched as an enlarged, more powerful, faster successor to the 1973 R90S which, with its small headlamp cowling, had been a big hit. BMW

LEFT: The R100RS was one of the most striking superbikes of 1976, primarily for it being the world's first motorcycle equipped with a full fairing. BMW

RIGHT: Although never intended as a track machine, the resulting improved aerodynamics and boosted power made the R100RS BMW's fastest yet. BMW

Styled by in-house designer Hans Muth, optimised aerodynamically in Pininfarina's wind tunnel and finished in a blue-ish sheen of silver metallic paint, the RS's striking fiberglass fairing, combined with its bigger engine to make the new bike BMW's fastest ever, at 125mph. What's more, slathered in metallic silver and equipped with BMW's new 'snowflake' alloy wheels, the RS was also one of the most stylish and modern-looking bikes of the era, too. And if you went for the optional, even sleeker, matching three-quarter seat, it looked even better still.

In truth, underneath the fancy fiberglass and plastic, and bigger numbers, the RS wasn't that remarkable. Yes, the engine was bigger, the chassis stronger and the bodywork mostly new, but the RS was still essentially a sober, sensible and expensive tourer rather than any kind of sports powerhouse. Even so, for covering vast distances at high speed there was little better; as a motorcycling status symbol nothing came close, as a mid-'70s poster bike and Top Trumps winner, the RS was up there with the best and no motorcycle fairing before or since is as recognisable as that of R100RS.

Futuristic, effective and exclusively expensive, the R100RS was the ultimate 'gentleman's express' for those wanting the best in long-range luxury. In the first ever readers'

to win the very first AMA Superbike championship in 1976 in the hands of ex-pat Brit Reg Pridmore.

That same year BMW went even further still. With the arrival of machines such as Honda's GL1000 Gold Wing and Kawasaki's new Z1000, it had become clear that the market trend was for ever-larger displacements so, after a production run of just three years, BMW's /6 series was replaced by the new, often enlarged /7 series. Along with the new R60/7 and R75/7, BMW introduced not just the new R100/7 (replacing the R90/6) with a full litre engine capacity, but also the stunning new R100RS.

Designed to be the Bavarian firm's new flagship, the R100RS was even more radical not for being the biggest boxer twin yet, or the most powerful (both of which it was, at 980cc and 70bhp respectively, having grown from the 898cc and 67bhp of 1973's R90S) but for being one of the first bikes designed to have a full fairing. And what a fairing it was!

SPECIFICATIONS

Price new	£3,300
Engine	980cc air-cooled boxer twin
Power	70bhp @ 7,000rpm
Torque	56lb-ft @ 6,000rpm
Frame	Tubular steel double cradle
Suspension	Telescopic forks (F), twin shocks (R)
Brakes	2 x 260mm discs (F), 200mm drum (R)
Tyres	3.25 x 19 (F), 4.00 x 18 (R)
Wet weight	230kg
Top speed	125mph

poll carried out by leading German motorcycle magazine *Motorrad*, the RS was voted 'Motorcycle of the Year'. It also remained in production for a full eight years right up to 1984, by which time over 30,000 had been sold.

Today, the 1976 R100RS remains arguably the 'ultimate' boxer, a '70s style icon popularised by celebrity riders such as comedian Dick Emery and *The Saint* star Ian Ogilvy and, also BMW's first superbike. Indeed, for a while, BMW in its own advertising claimed that the RS was 'The best superbike in the world'. And for a while at least, they were right... ■

1976 MOTO GUZZI
LE MANS 850

The Italian thoroughbred that was the poster bike for a generation

LEFT: Developed and enlarged from the earlier V7 Sport, Moto Guzzi's first Le Mans proved strikingly good looking, with fast and fine handling. PHIL WEST

Of all those versions, however, none are as much loved – or valuable – as that 1976 original. From today's perspective, the Mk1 Le Mans may be something of a wrist-straining 'tractor' with lumbering handling and performance, and crude build quality, but it also remains arguably the definitive 1970s Italian classic, with good ones now worth well over £10,000. ■

F ew superbike names have as much heritage, resonance and appeal as historic Italian marque Moto Guzzi's 1976 Mk 1 Le Mans.

Launched as an uprated, bikini faired, full sports version of the 'Grand Dame' of Italian motorcycling's previously ground-breaking 1971 V7 Sport, the Le Mans had it all in an age when Italian super/poster bikes still ruled the roost.

Conceived as a successor to the V7 Sport, the new bike was actually inspired by the company's successful endurance racing campaign in 1971 using a version of the V7. With an enlarged, 844cc version of its signature transverse V-twin, the racer led the Bol d'Or 24-hour race, then later led Le Mans for a full ten hours before finishing third – hence the road bike's name.

The production version's engine, however, was based on that of Guzzi's then T3 850 California tourer, tuned with high compression pistons, new cams and bigger 36mm Dell'Orto carburettors, with the result boosting peak power from 69 to 80bhp. To haul it all back down again, it also used the T3's new linked brakes which employed Brembo calipers and drilled cast iron discs.

A proper sports bike riding position was supplied via clip-on handlebars, rearset footrests and a humped seat. And to give it the style to match its sporting intent, it also gained a small, racy headlamp fairing and brazen livery, either in racing red or metallic blue.

The finished product, while still not quite as powerful or fast as the latest 'multis' from Japan, was still capable of 125mph, could see off all its European rivals, with the exception of the very best from Ducati and Laverda. It had fabulous, planted, lazy handling from its long and low chassis, and sounded and looked like nothing else. In short, the Le Mans looked great, went well, handled better, and had a bellowing soundtrack nothing outside Italy could match. No wonder it was so desirable.

It was also a huge hit, becoming the 'poster' bike for a new Italophile generation and a mainstay of Guzzi's range, living on through five 'marks' into the 1980s and '90s, and eventually growing to 1000cc.

SPECIFICATIONS

Price new	£2,000
Engine	844cc air-cooled 90° transverse V-twin
Power	80bhp @ 7,300rpm
Torque	58lb-ft @ 6,000rpm
Frame	Tubular steel double cradle
Suspension	35mm telescopic forks (F), twin shocks (R)
Brakes	2 x 300mm discs (F), 300mm disc (R)
Tyres	3.50 x 18 (F), 4.00 x 18 (R)
Wet weight	215kg
Top speed	126mph

BELOW: It was also continuously updated with styling and mechanical updates, including fairing lowers, and growing in capacity in its later years to 1000cc. PHIL WEST

1976 LAVERDA JOTA 1000

The race special triple that – briefly – was the fastest superbike of all

Of all the famous Italian manufacturers vying for supremacy during the first superbike era of the early to mid-1970s, with Moto Guzzi, Ducati and Benelli among them, one stood out for its constant stream of powerhouse big bore twins and triples – Laverda.

And of all the sublime and brutish Laverdas of that era, one machine rose to almost legendary status as the fastest and most desirable of all – the Jota 1000.

Launched in 1976, the big three-cylinder Italian monster was effectively a special; a British-built performance version of an already beastly machine. The 981cc 3C was launched in 1973. Then, in 1975, Laverda offered the 3C-E version ('E' for English version) with a performance exhaust that raised power from 68 to 75bhp, plus twin Brembo disc brakes. But with the ascendancy of the Avon Roadrunner production bike race series in the UK, British importers Slater Brothers decided to go even further and build a performance version in order to grab glory.

Performance cams and altered carburation took peak power up to 90bhp, a race seat, rear disc brake and five-spoke cast alloy wheels enhanced the chassis, racers could get a close-ratio gearbox, and the following year the new bike gained a name, that of an Italian dance in triple time – Jota.

That year, Pete Davies famously (through a series of subsequent Avon advertisements) rode the result to victory in the Avon championship. Just as importantly, the UK's *Motor Cycle Weekly* tested it at MIRA and posted a new record one-way top speed of 140.04mph (Kawasaki's previous Z1 900 had achieved 'just' 131), and a new superbike king was crowned.

In reality, of course, on the street the Jota was uncompromising, intimidating, expensive and extreme, and only really made sense when ridden fast. It was tall, heavy and unwieldy; it had a heavy clutch and a fickle ignition system. Its twin Brembo may have been state of the art, but it required a gorilla's grip to operate, and steering required sheer muscle.

As a symbolic performance king, no 1970s superbike came close. The Jota may have been a 'special' and been relatively short lived, but in terms of having Top Trumps-winning power, speed and race success, no bike did it better than the handsome, bright orange 'Beast from Breganze'.

Due to its origins and the creation of many replicas, production numbers are difficult to ascertain. But 'first year' Jotas remain among the most collectable of Italian classics, with prices often exceeding £15,000. ■

SPECIFICATIONS	
Price new	£2,250
Engine	981cc air-cooled DOHC transverse triple
Power	90bhp @ 8,000rpm
Torque	66lb-ft @ 7,000rpm
Frame	Tubular steel double cradle
Suspension	38mm telescopic forks (F), twin shocks (R)
Brakes	2 x 280mm discs (F), 280mm disc (R)
Tyres	100/90 x 18 (F), 120/90 x 18 (R)
Wet weight	220kg
Top speed	140mph

RIGHT: The tuned, big, three-cylinder engine helped make the Jota the fastest production motorcycle of the mid-1970s. PHIL WEST

BELOW: Although built by Italian manufacturer Laverda, the Jota 1000 was actually a British machine modified by importers Slater Brothers for racing. PHIL WEST

1978 SUZUKI GS1000

Suzuki's first 1000cc four which started a new superbike era

Suzuki truly came of age in the 1970s, first with the four-cylinder GS750 in 1976, the company's first four stroke after the debacle of the RE-5 rotary which followed the mostly smaller two strokes it had made its name with, and then, even more significantly, with the GS1000 and the four-valve GSXs that followed.

By the mid-1970s, with the 'Big Four' Japanese companies – Honda, Yamaha, Kawasaki and Suzuki – gaining increasing success with larger capacity machines, it was increasingly clear that bigger, multi cylinder, four-stroke bikes were the way to go.

Honda had paved the way with its SOHC four-cylinder CB750 in 1969, the machine which today is considered the first 'superbike'. Then Kawasaki raised the bar further with its DOHC, 903cc Z1 in 1972.

Ever since 1971, however, Suzuki's flagship had been a two stroke – the liquid cooled, three-cylinder GT750. In 1974, the manufacturer attempted to change direction and move away from 'strokers' with its larger bikes (partly due to ever tightening American emissions regulations) by creating a futuristic new flag bearer. The result was the radical, rotary engined RE-5, which, although warmly welcomed by the press, proved a sales disaster which almost sank the whole company.

In response, and desperate to get back on a more level footing, Suzuki then came up with the GS750. Although outwardly conventional in being a DOHC, two-valve four (and considered by some to be little more than a copy of Kawasaki's Z1 engine), Suzuki deliberately made it as reliable and refined as possible. It set a new standard for Japanese superbike handling and so was a truly landmark machine, marking the start of a new era.

The name, meanwhile – GS standing for 'Grand Sporting' – was

chosen to distinguish it from Suzuki's two stroke 'Grand Touring' GTs.

Hugely successful and fastidiously engineered, the 1976 GS750

ABOVE: The 1000 was effectively a larger version of the GS750 which was Suzuki's first four-cylinder four stroke and had been launched in 1976.
SUZUKI

LEFT: The GS1000E was launched in 1978 and proved an immediate hit both on road and track for combination of power and handling.
SUZUKI

ABOVE: While, finally, all were then superseded by a new, enlarged four-valve version (the FSs were two valve) headlined by the awesome GSX1100.
SUZUKI

SPECIFICATIONS

Price new	£1,725
Engine	987cc air-cooled DOHC transverse four
Power	90bhp @ 8,200rpm
Torque	61.5lb-ft @ 6,500rpm
Frame	Tubular steel double cradle
Suspension	Telescopic forks (F), twin shocks (R)
Brakes	2 x 295mm discs (F), 295mm disc (R)
Tyres	3.50 x 19 (F), 4.50 x 17 (R)
Dry weight	232kg
Top speed	137mph

became the basis for a family of GS successors. A smaller GS550 arrived in 1977, which proved popular as a junior superbike. And in 1978, the GS1000 landed and became an instant success when, according to bikesport folklore, the legendary 'Pops' Yoshimura in just 50 days tuned the bike which was ridden to victory in the 1978 Daytona Superbike race by Steve McLaughlin. Later that year came victory at the prestigious Suzuka 8 Hours with the legendary Wes Cooley on board, while Cooley would also go on to win the 1979 and 1980 AMA titles, successes that spawned the GS1000S 'Cooley Replica'.

Based on the already brilliant 750, the GS1000 fundamentally changed the perceptions of what 'UJM's – Universal Japanese Motorcycles – the disparaging term commonly then used for the new breed of transversely mounted, four-cylinder Japanese superbikes which were fast but also heavy and poor handling – were capable of.

Although similar to the GS750, the 1000's larger, 997cc, two valve, four-cylinder engine was also lighter and shorter, largely due to its crank having non-circular 'webs' rather than full flywheels, also doing without the 750's kickstarter and shaft.

On top of that, although a full-size machine with fairly generic 'UJM' styling, the GS1000 was lighter than its Japanese rivals, had a comparatively stiff chassis and benefitted from quality air-assisted forks and adjustable rear shocks.

The result was not just a class-leading 90bhp making the GS

easily capable of 130mph, but also, for the first time, had the assured handling and cornering ability to match. It was all enough to make the new GS1000 not just the new king on the street but on track as well, winning both the 1978 Daytona 200 and Suzuka 8 Hours, and going on to win the 1979 AMA Superbike championship.

But more was still to come. Although Suzuki's new GS1000 four was fast, fine-handling and fabulous value, it lacked the style and sheer visual drama of, say, Kawasaki's 1979 Z1-R. The 1980 GS1000S was created to change all that. Although fundamentally a standard GS1000, the S gave the GS a racy pzazz the standard bike didn't have. A limited-edition machine intended to homologate performance features for Cooley's 1980 campaign, it became the first production Suzuki to feature a fairing (a stylish, handlebar design which also gained a clock), a larger 18in rear wheel (compared to the previous

> ## 66 The GS1000 became an instant success 99

17in version) uprated suspension, and Suzuki racing livery in either white/blue or white/red.

Unveiled at the end of 1979, the S, with the suffix signifying 'Sport', was an instant sensation, went on to power Cooley to a second title in 1980 (so inspiring the 'Wes Cooley replica' nickname it acquired), and was immediately the most desirable – Honda CBX arguably aside – of all Japanese UJMs. That mantle may not have lasted long – Suzuki's own first four-valve GSX1100 debuted later in 1980 – but in the final year of the 1970s, the GS1000S was one of the most loved motorcycles of all.

Suzuki's next major development came in 1980 when the two-valve GS1000 was replaced by an enlarged, four-valve version, which also incorporated Suzuki's new Twin Swirl Combustion Chamber (TSCC) technology. To mark this, the new bike was given the 'X' designation, which reputedly stood for 'eXperimental'. The first, the GSX1100, with a genuine 100bhp and 140mph potential, was the most powerful, fastest bike of its day, again spawning a whole family of Suzuki four-valve GSXs ranging from twin cylinder 250s and 400s, to 400, 550 and 750 fours and more.

Even more than that, however, the GSX then developed into a radical and varied range of bikes. That first GSX1100 led to 1981's radical, futuristically styled GSX1100S Katana. In 1984, Suzuki came up with the fully faired GSX1100EF tourer. There was also the half-faired GSX1100ES of 1983, the later roadster, shaft-drive GSX1100G, and many more. In short, if you wanted a multi cylinder four-stroke Suzuki in the early 1980s, you wanted a GSX. ■

BELOW: Other variants followed, including the gorgeous, half-faired sports version, the GS1000S, which debuted in 1979.
SUZUKI

Every so often Honda flexes its engineering muscles. In the 1970s it came up with the oval-pistoned NR500 GP racer; in the '80s the CX500 Turbo, and in the 1990s the road going NR750. But it was the 1978 CBX which was arguably the Japanese firm's greatest tour de force.

Conceived in early 1976 following the initial failure of the GoldWing, inspired by Honda's incredible 1966 250cc, six-cylinder RC166 GP racer, and launched in 1978 to mark ten years since Honda's original CB750 superbike, the CBX was not only the world's first mass production six-cylinder motorcycle (Benelli's earlier Sei was never mass production) but also its most outrageous and powerful.

With Japanese rivals Suzuki and Yamaha also beginning to explore 750cc four-strokes (with their upcoming GS and XS750s, respectively), Kawasaki established as the superbike king with its Z900 and new Z650, its own SOHC CB750 now outpaced and yet with a 1960s four-stroke racing legacy of five and even six-cylinder machines, Honda decided to re-establish its superbike supremacy with the 'ultimate' CB.

After considering a four-cylinder 1000 and 1200, an all-new, litre-class six designed by Soichiro Irimajiri (the man behind those '60s racers) was chosen. The four-cylinder concept, meanwhile, was continued by another team to become the 1979 CB900F.

The result, with 1048cc and 105bhp, was the biggest and most powerful bike of the time. And, with double overhead cams, four valves per cylinder and six exquisite 28mm

With its six-cylinder CBX1000 Honda's was not so much raising the bar of what a superbike was capable of, as flexing its technological muscles. HONDA

1978 HONDA CBX1000

The biggest, boldest superbike of the 1970s... but not the best

carburettors, it was also the most sophisticated. A tubular spine frame was settled on as it would show the engine at its best. It had 35mm forks, disc brakes all round, and Honda's latest pressed aluminium Comstar wheels.

The CBX had its world press launch at the Suzuka race circuit, Japan, in November 1977, production machines arrived in UK dealers March 1978, and some of the first examples were used by travelling marshals at that year's TT – the one when Honda legend Mike Hailwood returned to grab his fairytale win.

Despite all the positive publicity, the CBX was a slow seller and not a commercial success. It cost an enormous £2,750 when Suzuki's class-leading GS1000E was £1,000 less, and its performance and complexity meant few insurance companies would provide cover.

In 1979 Honda added to their own woes by launching the 'four-cylinder alternative' – the CB900F with 95bhp, more agile handling and similarly cheaper price, and by

BELOW: Expensive and complex, the CBX was never a sales success (especially as Honda's own CB900F was cheaper and faster), but it remains a superbike icon. HONDA

year's end unsold CBXs were being discounted by as much as £1,000.

Reinvented as a faired, panniered, monoshock tourer for 1981, the CBX limped on before finally being deleted in 1982. Commercially it had been a failure but as a statement, flagship, technical tour de force, no bike did it better, and today the mad, magnificent CBX remains one of the most prized Japanese classics of all. ■

SPECIFICATIONS	
Price new	£2,699
Engine	1047cc air-cooled DOHC transverse six
Power	105bhp @ 9,000rpm
Torque	61lb-ft @ 8,000rpm
Frame	Tubular steel, engine stressed member
Suspension	35mm telescopic forks (F), twin shocks (R)
Brakes	2 x 265mm discs (F), 265mm disc (R)
Tyres	3.50 x 19 (F), 4.25 x 18 (R)
Dry weight	233kg
Top speed	135mph

ABOVE: Ducati's second 'racer replica' (after the 750 SuperSports) was based on the then 900 Supersport but effectively with different bodywork. DUCATI

On June 2, 1978, one of motorcycle's greatest fairy tales took place on the demanding roads of the Isle of Man TT. Legendary multiple world champion Mike 'The Bike' Hailwood, who'd retired from racing 11 years previously, returned to compete at the ripe old age of 38 and, aboard a privately entered, twin-cylinder Ducati 'David' against a works four-cylinder Honda 'Goliath' ridden by 1974 500cc champion Phil Read, won the Formula One race.

That stunning 'comeback' victory remains one of the most celebrated motorcycle sporting accomplishments, not just of the '70s but of all time.

In the 1960s, Hailwood had been one of the world's most successful racers, riding for the likes of MV Agusta and Honda. Over those years he won nine world championships, 76 grand prix, and lived a playboy lifestyle. In 1967, however, in response to new regulations which banned its six-cylinder engines, Honda pulled out of GP racing and paid Hailwood £50,000 to not ride for any other team. Hailwood thereafter took only one-off rides, including for BSA/Triumph at the 1970 Daytona 200, then turned to car racing, before retiring to New Zealand in 1974.

In 1978, however, after trying out and being impressed by a Ducati V-twin the previous year, he accepted an offer from UK dealer Sports Motorcycles to ride a Ducati in the new TT F1 race. Although a production-based formula, Hailwood's bike

1979 DUCATI MHR900

The Italian racer replica that honoured Mike Hailwood's finest hour

was a racing machine by Italian specialists NCR with a lightweight frame but was still significantly down on power compared to Read's 750cc four-cylinder Honda, and Hailwood himself hadn't raced on the Isle of Man for 11 years, so his victory caused a sensation.

The following year, Ducati capitalised on his victory by launching a replica, the 1979 MHR (Mike Hailwood Replica) 900. It looked the part, too, being a 900cc V-twin with full race fairing and copycat tank/seat in Hailwood red, green and white and with uprated rear suspension, clocks and switches. An initial 500 were built (by NCR), selling out instantly and prompting Ducati to turn it into a full production machine for 1980.

In truth, the fairy tale wasn't quite so perfect. The first MHR was little more than Ducati's 900SS in different bodywork, but the 1980 version featured a modified fairing, the 1981 different exhausts, and the 1982 new side panels, by which time it had become Ducati's best-selling model.

By then, too, the fairy tale had turned sour. Hailwood had returned

to the TT the following year, this time coming second in the F1 race Ducati but winning the Senior on a Suzuki, before retiring for good. In 1981 he was killed in a car accident in while taking his children to get fish and chips.

Production of the MHR, meanwhile, finally ended in 1986. In truth, none were the performance specials their name and style suggested, but in 1979, as an iconic Italian superbike with incomparable racing pedigree, nothing came close. ■

BELOW: Instead of Imola, it was inspired by Mike Hailwood's stunning 'comeback' victory for Ducati at the 1978 F1 Isle of Man TT. DUCATI

SPECIFICATIONS

Price new	£2,999
Engine	864cc air-cooled 90° desmodromic V-twin
Power	80bhp @ 7,500rpm
Torque	63.5lb-ft @ 5,800rpm
Frame	Tubular steel, engine stressed member
Suspension	38mm telescopic forks (F), twin shocks (R)
Brakes	2 x 280mm discs (F), 280mm disc (R)
Tyres	100/90 x 18 (F), 120/90 x 18 (R)
Dry weight	205kg
Top speed	137mph

1980 SUZUKI GSX1100S KATANA

The first boldly styled superbike which broke the mould of UJMs

There's little doubt that one of the most significant names in Japanese superbike model history is that of the revolutionary Suzuki Katana.

Like both the Ninja from rivals Kawasaki or GSX-R from compatriots Suzuki, both of which were to follow, the Katana was not just one model or machine but a whole family of bikes over a wide range of different capacities. And like those, the Katana was not just a category of machine but a whole new design ethos.

Unlike the Kawasaki and Suzuki, however, the Katana was also very specific to a period of history: the early eighties. Or at least it was until its revival as a retro-inspired machine based on the then GSX-S1000 roadster in 2019...

That significance is down to a wide range of factors: first, and most obviously, the 1980 GSX1100S Katana (to give the original its full name) looked, with its sharp angles, blended-in bodywork and space-age silver livery, simply like literally nothing else. That alone, in the space age era of the early 1980s, of *Star Wars*, *Close Encounters* and *Buck Rogers*, made Suzuki's futuristic newcomer stand out even more.

Second, with the original 1100 flagged by Suzuki as the 'world's fastest production motorcycle', the first Katana also had performance credibility to back up its bold cosmetics.

The whole family of Katanas that followed, ranging from more accessible middleweights like the GS650G shaft-drive roadster and the similar, and even more affordable 550, to the even more exotic 'homologation special' GSX1000S

SPECIFICATIONS	
Price new	£2,850
Engine	1,075cc air-cooled DOHC transverse four
Power	100bhp @ 8,500rpm
Torque	67lb-ft @ 6,500rpm
Frame	Tubular steel double cradle
Suspension	37mm telescopic forks (F), twin shocks (R)
Brakes	2 x 275mm discs (F), 275mm disc (R)
Tyres	3.50 x 19 (F), 4.50 x 17 (R)
Dry weight	232kg
Top speed	140mph

ABOVE: It may have been based on largely unchanged GSX1100 mechanics, but the radically styled Suzuki Katana looked fast and that was arguably all that mattered. SUZUKI

LEFT: The angular fairing and radical front mudguard and more were created by German styling house Target Design on commission from Suzuki Germany. SUZUKI

ABOVE: The silver livery, suede-style seat, racing riding position and more were created to conspicuously break away from the then norm of the 'Universal Japanese Motorcycle'. SUZUKI

BELOW: 'Katana' also applied to more than just one bike. Although the 1100 was the flagship, there was also a milder 550, 650 and a racing 1000 special. SUZUKI

production racer (complete with Mikuni smoothbore carburettors), to the last 'true' original Katana, 1984's GSX750S3 with its distinctive, 'pop-up' headlamp, gave the Katana family a breadth, a performance pedigree and a technological significance that, overall, was massively influential. What's more, elements of 'Katana style' didn't just dribble down across Suzuki's whole range in the early '80s, it lives on even to this day. Blended-in seats, side panels and tanks, to give just one example, are all part of the Katana's design legacy.

How the Katana came about is just as significant. Throughout the 1970s, Japanese superbikes had largely followed a uniform design and styling template. Honda's original superbike, the single-cam CB750 of 1968, led to Kawasaki's 1972 DOHC Z1 900 then Suzuki's 1977 GS750 and GSX1100, and so on. From a distance, as upright, unfaired roadsters with transverse, multi cylinder engines, these UJMs (Universal Japanese Motorcycles as they became derided) all looked the same.

That fundamentally changed for the first time with the Katana. From 1980-1985 if you wanted a Suzuki capable of sending shivers down your spine you wanted a Katana, either on your bedroom wall or, preferably, on your garage floor. No Suzuki – no motorcycle even – not before or since, had been so striking. And the Katana still is today.

And yet it nearly didn't happen at all.

Commissioned initially by Suzuki as a one-off 'design exercise', a concept bike was first displayed in 1979 and public reaction was so great that the Katana ended up being much, much more. Concept bikes don't usually make it into production, after all – they're too wild for that. And even when they do, as with Yamaha's much later MT-01 or Suzuki's own B-King, they usually end up being sales flops. The Katana, however, named, after a Japanese warrior's sword, was very different.

In fact, the Katana was different from the off – in being the first Japanese motorcycle styled by an external design house. In the late 1970s, Suzuki had become concerned about the stagnating design of the UJMs of the era and wanted to make its bikes stand out with what it called 'a European-type design'. And, with its European HQ being in Germany, Suzuki Germany's marketing manager, Manfred Becker, turned to newly formed German stylist company, Target Design, to come up with the goods.

Target, comprising founder Hans-Georg Kasten, Jan Fellstrom and Hans Muth (who had mostly been involved with BMW cars), had first sprung to prominence with a restyled MV Agusta of all things that bore a striking resemblance to the subsequent Katanas which they had created in association with, and was published by, German magazine *Motorrad*. But the Suzuki commission enabled Target, and particularly Fellstrom (the main creative force behind the Katana), to take those ideas further still.

Suzuki's first commission was for a sportier version of its 650cc four cylinder shaft-drive roadster. Target's result was the ED-1 650 (ED standing for European Design), which later became the GS650G and GS550 Katanas. Suzuki Japan, meanwhile, was sufficiently impressed to quickly follow this up with a second commission for a top-of-the-line sports model based on its then class-leading superbike, the GSX1100. The half-faired ED-2 1100 (which would become the production GSX1100S) was what Target came up with next.

And it is this latter bike, as first shown at the Cologne Show in Germany in the autumn of 1979, which was the official start of the whole Katana sensation. It had a radical, angular purity ranging from its wedge shape, frame-mounted fairing (at that time without a screen and conceived to ensure the stability at speed that Suzuki requested), faired-in side panels and a stumpy, dual-textured short seat. The new prototype,

although based on an unchanged GSX1100 16 valve, air-cooled engine, tubular steel, double cradle frame, twin shock rear suspension, and other cycle parts including its cast aluminium wheels, was simply show stoppingly different.

In fact, Suzuki was so emboldened by the public's reaction that it decided to put both the milder 650/500 and the wilder 1100, immediately into production. And the rest, as they say, is history.

Impressively, the production Katanas differed only slightly from the prototypes, with the changes including a small wind deflector screen (as insisted upon by Suzuki), paired silencers instead of Muth's four-into-one, and black accent paint on the front mudguard and airbox covers.

Target's design philosophy – of keeping components compact and close-fitting – had been applied to all areas of the bike's design which also had the beneficial effect of reducing weight, the number of components required, and thus production costs. Further examples of this approach included the dramatically simple instrument cluster with overlapping dials and its offset fuel cap, which allowed for a clean continuous seam weld on the tank.

Suzuki's bold performance claims also proved to be accurate

> **66 The Katana remained hugely significant 99**

and attractive. In comparative track testing, *Cycle Canada* magazine recorded a top speed of 237km/h (147mph) for the 1100 Katana against 227km/h (141mph) for the standard GSX1100E. The next fastest was the 1982 Kawasaki GPz1100 at 225km/h (140mph) followed by the ageing Laverda Mirage 1200 at 222km/h (138mph).

ABOVE: If ever there was a motorcycle which didn't need the addition of a period 'dolly bird' to grab your eye, the Katana was surely it! SUZUKI

BELOW: Clever design details, meanwhile, included a fuel tap integrated into the left-hand side panel, and overlapping clocks in the slimline dash. SUZUKI

"Fast though the Katana is," *MCN* wrote in its first road test in March 1980, "I suspect people will buy one more to be different than anything else. The styling is a poseur's dream and when riding through town it's hard to resist a crafty look at yourself as you pass plateglass windows."

Nor was the 1100 the only 'fast' Katana. A special, the GSX1000S arrived soon after to satisfy homologation purposes for production-based racing in the US and UK. By decreasing the 1100's bore by 2.6mm, displacement was reduced to 998cc. It also

featured flat-slide carburettors where the 1100 had conventional CVs, a performance inlet camshaft and was often fitted with optional wire wheels, which were lighter and –with an 18in rear – allowed tyre choices which were more suitable for the track. Just 3,000 were produced, the bikes won production racing series in both the US and UK, and with few survivors, they're now the most collectable – and valuable – Katanas of all.

In truth, the 1100 in particular, wasn't a huge sales success as just as many were also put off by those extreme looks and the Katana's relatively high price – but nor was it a disaster, either. And while the 1100 had already been deleted by 1983, its brief, shining existence, the popularity of the more subtle 650 and 550 versions, and Suzuki's persistence in applying 'watered-down' elements of the Katana design across its whole range in the early '80s (everything from the GS125 to the GSX550 to the GSX1100 retained shades of Katana design for years to come), meant the Katana remained hugely significant.

Nor did it all end quite as suddenly as Suzuki had intended, either. The Katana family had been conceived to give Suzuki's air-cooled GSX sportsters added style. With the GSX made redundant by the first oil-cooled racer replica GSX-R in 1985, the Katana's job, you might have thought, was done and production was duly ended. Except... it didn't quite work out that way.

First, in the US, Suzuki retained the Katana name by applying it to all manner of arguably less-deserving machines such as the GSX600F 'teapot' and GSX750F.

Second, Suzuki itself then revived the original 1100 Katana when, in 1990, to celebrate the Hamamatsu company's 70th anniversary, it took the unprecedented step of 'remanufacturing' a batch of 200 Katana 1100s in totally original 1980 specification for sale on the home, Japanese market. This proved so successful that Suzuki repeated the operation the following year, while later versions were also remanufactured (primarily again for the domestic Japanese market and with a few modifications) right up to 2001.

Third, spurred on by these bikes' popularity, Suzuki the same year (1991) then pre-empted the current fashion for 'retro' bikes by a full 20 years by producing (again for the domestic Japanese market) a 250cc, four-cylinder Katana replica based on the then Bandit 250. This was also then followed up with a 400cc version, both of which occasionally became available in the UK as grey imports.

All of that combines to contribute to the Katana's significance, its popularity, and its legacy.

The original GSX1100S Katana itself may have had limited sales success, been something of a 'Marmite machine' and fairly short lived, but the Katana story

as a whole simply has it all. The first 1100 had earth-shattering looks and the 'world's fastest' tag. The 1000cc special version was the championship-winning production racer; the 550, 650, 750 and later 400s were the bikes of the masses, and the later reproductions only added to the classic allure.

Today, those original big bore bikes, the 1100 and particularly the race spec 1000, are as bone fide a Japanese classic as they get, with prices for the latter peaking at well over £10,000. But a 400 or 550, or even a bike such as a GSX750ES, which still has shades of Katana style, can still be had for relative peanuts.

And they're all still a tempting, striking and significant motorcycle, too. It may be true that none of those original Katanas were a commercial success. The 1100 was divisive and expensive, the middleweights proved 'Marmite' motorcycles, and by 1985, with the introduction of Suzuki's first GSX-R, all Katanas in Europe suddenly seemed obsolete and were summarily dropped.

But the name lived on, particularly in the US, revival versions in 1100, 400 and 250cc forms, were made in the '90s, the original is today a true mould-breaking classic and after the Katana, no Japanese motorcycle looked the same. Or, to put it another way, without the Katana, the first Japanese superbike to take bold styling seriously, we might still all be riding boring old UJMs... ■

The early 1980s was an era of rapid development for Japanese superbikes after years of similar, four-cylinder, twin shock machines such as Kawasaki's Z1 and Suzuki's GS1000E which gave rise to the term Universal Japanese Motorcycle (UJM).

Suzuki was the first to buck the conformity with its radically styled Katana of 1980. But Kawasaki was next with its first GPz, the 1100B1, in 1981.

Based on the Z1000J1, the GPz's engine was enlarged to 1089cc to become the biggest 'Z' yet, and given fuel injection, the result being a class-leading 108bhp and 137mph, and the best acceleration in its class. Just as significant was the GPz's brazen new image, with distinctive red livery, contrasting black/silver stripes and, instead of the usual silver engine and chrome detailing, black engines, exhausts, and fork sliders.

That first GPz1100 was also quickly followed by a whole family of GPzs, including a tuned 550 then a 750, both with distinctive nose fairings. An aggressive advertising campaign underlining the trio's performance with the slogan 'Who Can Catch a Kawasaki?' further emphasised the new GPz family's performance.

The success of those bikes was then followed by a flurry of model updates that underlined the GPzs' significance, including the 1100B1 becoming the B2 in 1982 with a cockpit fairing similar to the 550 and 750, new LCD warning lights and improved suspension, and all

1981 KAWASAKI
GPz1100

Three little letters that changed the whole course of superbike evolution

culminating with the 'Unitrak' GPzs from 1983.

After the first GPz1100B1 rewrote the superbike rulebook in 1981, its successor, the GPz1100A1, redefined 1980s superbikes once again.

This 'second generation' GPz1100 gained a mildly reworked engine which raised power from 108 to 120bhp but even more significant was its new monoshock rear suspension dubbed 'Unitrak' to go with swoopy, all-new styling including a frame-mounted half-fairing.

The curvy, low-slung look was carried across all Kawasaki GPzs (the 305, 550, 750 and 1100) that year. The riding position was lower and sportier, and the improved aerodynamics, combined with the power increase, was enough for the GPz1100 to hit 140mph and so regain its crown as the fastest superbike of the day.

That 'day' however, was once again short lived. Almost as soon as the GPz1100A1 was unveiled in 1983, Honda also introduced

its first liquid-cooled V4s, the VF750S then F, which effectively sounded the final death knell for the 1970s-style, air cooled, two-valve four. The GPz11 limped on for a second year in 1984 as the GPz1100B2, but its days were numbered. Kawasaki itself was about to launch its own all-new superbike, the GPz900R, which would quickly consign the big Unitraks to history. Until then, however, the big, brash and brilliant GPz1100 was as fast and sexy as superbikes got. ■

ABOVE: Kawasaki first came up with its enlarged, tuned, brazen GPz1100 in 1981. This faired successor, the B2, arrived the following year. KAWASAKI

BELOW: But even more radical was the swoopy-styled, Unitrak A1 of 1983, which was the fastest bike of the era when initially launched. KAWASAKI

SPECIFICATIONS (B1)

Price new	£2,649
Engine	1,098cc air-cooled DOHC transverse four
Power	108bhp @ 8,000rpm
Torque	70lb-ft @ 7,000rpm
Frame	Tubular steel double cradle
Suspension	38mm telescopic forks (F), twin shocks (R)
Brakes	2 x 275mm discs (F), 275mm disc (R)
Tyres	3.25 x 18 (F), 4.25 x 18 (R)
Dry weight	237kg
Top speed	137mph

1984 HONDA VF1000R

The best example from Honda's early new V4 superbike era

W hen superbikes transformed in the early-to-mid 1980s from air cooled, twin shock fours (such as Kawasaki's first GPz1100), into a new breed of liquid-cooled, monoshock machines, the manufacturer leading the way, although initially not entirely successfully, was Honda.

The Japanese giant's concept for this brave new world was for a liquid-cooled V4 – and not just one, but a whole range of bikes ranging from 400 to 1100cc. The first was the 1982 VF750S followed by the flawed VF750F, and a 400 in 1983. But the best – and Honda's new V4 flagship – was the VF1000R, as launched in Europe in March 1984. A more straightforward VF1000F was also launched around the same time.

Although on face value the 1000R was a sports version of the F, there was much more to it than that. With production-based racing shifting from 1000cc to a 750cc formula in 1983, the R was never intended for

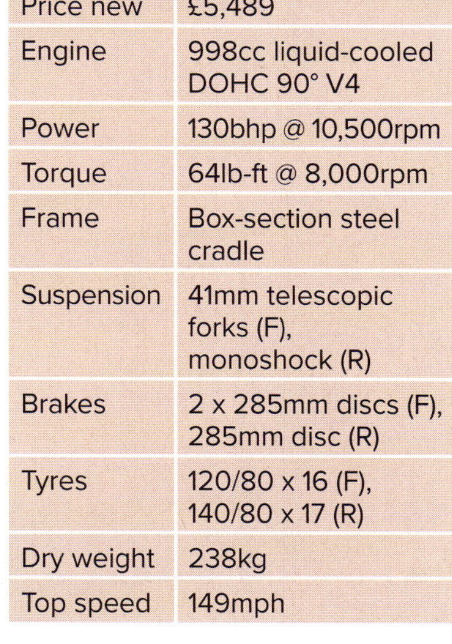

Honda had earlier launched the 1982 VF750S and, in 1983, this VF750F sportster but, although quick, it was plagued with cam problems. HONDA

racing. Instead, it was conceived to be a road-going replica of Honda's 1982 V4 FWS1000 F1 racer which won both that year's AMA F1 championship and, in the hands of Joey Dunlop, the TT, and was intended to be the 'ultimate VF', showcasing Honda's latest technology.

As such, the R's engine, for example, had a complex and heavy gear-driven camtrain instead of the

F's chain, plus different crank and high compression heads producing 122bhp. And although the R's box-section frame and monoshock were also from the F, the anti-dive front forks were an upgrade, the brakes improved, and wheels uprated to race-style bolt-together Comstars most recently seen on American motorcycle racer Freddie Spencer's GP500.

But the biggest change was to its image and bodywork, with the R gaining twin radiators and race-style bodywork comprising a full fairing, removable seat hump and twin endurance-style headlights (a year before Suzuki's new GSX-R750) all in classic Honda racing colours of red, white and blue.

The result was enough to drive the VF-R onto 150mph, making it the fastest bike of the day (until Kawasaki's new GPz900R arrived shortly after), the most exotic Japanese superbike ever, and a true poster-worthy machine.

Unfortunately, all that tech and the gear-driven cams also made the R heavy (50kg more than Kawasaki's GPz900R), and without any real race wins it was something of a white elephant plus, at £5,489 in 1984, it was also ridiculously expensive, so was never a sales success.

Production limped on through two subtle revisions up to 1986 with unsold, discounted examples by then going for a song. Yet in its day, the VF1000R was the greatest and fastest superbike Japan had ever produced and a machine without which Honda would have never produced the brilliant VFR750F and RC30 yet to come. ■

BELOW: The VF1000R was the highlight of Honda's initial foray into V4 powerplants but although glorious, fast and sophisticated, it wasn't a success. HONDA

SPECIFICATIONS	
Price new	£5,489
Engine	998cc liquid-cooled DOHC 90° V4
Power	130bhp @ 10,500rpm
Torque	64lb-ft @ 8,000rpm
Frame	Box-section steel cradle
Suspension	41mm telescopic forks (F), monoshock (R)
Brakes	2 x 285mm discs (F), 285mm disc (R)
Tyres	120/80 x 16 (F), 140/80 x 17 (R)
Dry weight	238kg
Top speed	149mph

THE DESTINATION FOR
CLASSIC VEHICLE ENTHUSIASTS

Visit us today and discover all our latest releases

Order from our online shop...
shop.keypublishing.com/specials
Call +44 (0)1780 480404 *(Monday to Friday 9am - 5.30pm GMT)*
**Free 2nd class P&P on BFPO orders. Overseas charges apply.*

1984 YAMAHA FJ1100

The bike with which Yamaha first joined the Japanese superbike elite

Yamaha's first large capacity superbike was the air-cooled FJ1100 but although capable and with fine handling, it was quickly outpaced by Kawasaki's new GPz900R. YAMAHA

The big FJ soldiered on before being recategorised as a sports tourer, in which form it lived on for a decade. YAMAHA

Although launched as a capable, sporty superbike, today Yamaha's big, faired FJ isn't remembered as one. Instead, as it was quickly overshadowed by Kawasaki's all-new lighter, faster GPz900R, the FJ1100 was quickly redefined as a sports tourer and, when later updated to become the FJ1200, it was probably the best of the breed – not just in the 1980s but through most of the 1990s as well.

The FJ's air-cooled DOHC four was inspired by that of the preceding XS1100 four and, before that, the 1978 XS750 triple, which had been Yamaha's first big four stroke 'multi'. Featuring 16 valves and relatively narrow dimensions due to the positioning of its alternator behind the cylinders, its whopping 1097ccs produced an equally massive 125bhp with the torque to match, the highest of the day.

Even more significant, though, was the FJ1100's chassis. Conceived to keep the centre of gravity low, despite the sheer bulk of the engine, its frame was a pioneering 'perimeter' design, whereby frame tubes wrapped around the engine instead of it being cradled from below or suspended from above. These tubes were also in box-section (rather than round) steel, and Yamaha dubbed the whole design the 'Lateral/Perimeter Frame Concept'.

The pioneering 'tech' did not end there: monoshock rear suspension worked a beefy, box-section aluminium swing arm; there were small, nimble 16in wheels both front and rear; its brakes employed novel ventilated twin discs, plus there was a swoopy, frame-mounted half-fairing which both protected the rider and left the engine exposed to the cooling wind flow.

The result, although fast with fine handling, was also quickly exposed by the GPz900R as being heavy – 556lb compared to the Kawasaki's 502lb. Unusually, however, that also very soon didn't seem to matter. The FJ1100 was also smooth, immensely stable and comfortable – all sports-touring virtues which were consolidated by its 1986 successor. That bike, the FJ1200, produced 130bhp and quickly became established as one of the decade's most popular sports tourers. Then, for 1989 it was updated again with a more precise-steering, 17in front wheel, uprated four-piston brakes and more protective bodywork, and its superiority in the class was underlined, living on well into the mid-1990s.

The FJ1100 may have never quite been a dominant superbike, but by the end of the 1980s and then well into the 1990s, it certainly became the 'king' it had always promised to be – but as a sports tourer rather than sportster. ■

SPECIFICATIONS

Price new	£3,500
Engine	1097cc air-cooled DOHC transverse four
Power	125bhp @ 9,000rpm
Torque	64.2lb-ft @ 8,000rpm
Frame	Box-section steel cradle
Suspension	41mm telescopic forks (F), monoshock (R)
Brakes	2 x 282mm discs (F), 282mm disc (R)
Tyres	120/80 x 16 (F), 150/80 x 16 (R)
Dry weight	227kg
Top speed	146mph

When it was unveiled, the all-new Kawasaki GPz900R caused a sensation. Intended as the successor to the Z1 900, it proved equally revolutionary. KAWASAKI

1984 KAWASAKI
GPz900R NINJA

The Z1 successor that changed the superbike 'template' forever

The GPz900R Ninja is probably not only the most significant Kawasaki motorcycle model of the last 50 years, but almost certainly the most influential motorcycle over the same period. It set the template for the modern superbike, became the longest-lived Kawasaki model of all time, and was the first to be given the iconic 'Ninja' moniker. And that was just the start.

The GPz900R was so good it outlived not one but TWO of its supposed successors, dominated big bike production racing at the Isle of Man, starred in a blockbuster Hollywood movie and sold more as an individual model than most motorcycle manufacturers do in total in a single year. Simply, modern superbikes don't get any more 'legendary' and deservingly celebrated than the GPz900R.

Looking back at its launch from over 40 years distant, it's hard, if not impossible, for most to remember the fundamental 'sea change' moment the Ninja's

arrival represented. Simply, it was like jumping forward in time. In 1980, the benchmark big bike was Suzuki's new GSX1100, which, despite new four-valve, 'Twin Swirl' heads, fundamentally had the same air-cooling, twin shocks and naked, tubular steel cradle frame

all motorcycles had had since the 1950s. The all-new GPz, however, was different – very different.

And it was the result of one of the longest and most ambitious development processes in motorcycle history...

By the late 1970s, Kawasaki's air cooled, four cylinder, two-valve superbikes, such as the Z1000, were overdue a successor. All had been derived from 1973's Z1 900 and Kawasaki's experience of that bike when it had been beaten to the title of 'the world's first four-cylinder

SPECIFICATIONS

Price new	£3,199
Engine	908cc liquid-cooled DOHC transverse four
Power	115bhp @ 9,000rpm
Torque	63lb-ft @ 8,500rpm
Frame	Tubular steel spine
Suspension	39mm telescopic forks (F), monoshock (R)
Brakes	2 x 280mm discs (F), 270mm disc (R)
Tyres	120/80 x 16 (F), 130/80 x 18 (R)
Dry weight	228kg
Top speed	150mph

BELOW: It became the overnight flagship for a whole family of GPzs now ranging from 305 to 1100cc and even a Turbo – and the centre of Kawasaki's marketing. KAWASAKI

ABOVE: One of the first superbikes to be conceived as a whole, the GPz900R took a full seven years to develop and shared only its wheel design with previous models. KAWASAKI

750cc superbike' by Honda's 1968 CB750, so forcing its own, then imminent 750, back to the drawing board, and Kawasaki to raise the bar even higher. That machine would be the 1984 GPz900R Ninja, was developed in total secrecy over a full seven full years, when most new motorcycles of that era required only three.

At its heart was an all-new, liquid cooled, double overhead cam, 16 valve, transversely-arranged four cylinder which, like the Z1, was also 900cc (908, actually). But in every other respect, the new engine was a monumental advance from not just Kawasaki's previous air-cooled, eight-valve fours, but also all its rivals. In 1984 Yamaha and Suzuki were still labouring with their air-cooled two and four-valvers, while Honda's new liquid-cooled VF750 V4s had already proved to be flawed.

Of course, such a significantly advanced engine doesn't happen overnight. At the start of the project, Kawasaki first considered a DOHC six akin to its then in-development Z1300, before dismissing due to its width and weight. Honda-style V4s and V6s were also proposed, while Kawasaki even looked at upgrading the air-cooled motors then being used in the likes of its Z1000 (and later GPz750 and 1100s). Ultimately, however, in 1978, the decision was made to design an all-new motor. The result, six years later, was motorcycling's first production liquid-cooled, 16-valve, DOHC, inline four.

That liquid-cooled element was crucial: as well as allowing the

precise temperature management required for tighter tolerances and thus higher performance, it also, with the combination of a novel, side-mounted cam-chain, allowed the new motor to be light and compact. At 451mm wide, the new GPz900R engine was 20% narrower than all similar big fours of before.

And that, of course, was just the start. Kawasaki's new flagship was also pioneering in being the first superbike conceived as an integrated 'whole', with the new engine also used as a 'stressed

member'. This meant the engine worked within the new diamond steel frame and aluminium rear sub-frame as a centralised mass unit, so allowing greatly reduced weight and in turn improving the bike's handling, acceleration, braking and top speed. Although not a new idea – racing teams had been using the practice for some time – Kawasaki was the first to use it on a mass-produced road machine.

This integrated approach also led to another first – the GPz900R's aerodynamic full fairing, which in turn helped it towards a groundbreaking 150mph-plus top speed. Other advances included pioneering electronic ignition and a lightweight box section swing arm with fancy but effective eccentric chain adjusters.

The new Ninja wasn't all radical, though. The GPz900R's cycle parts, for example, were largely conventional. The Uni-Trak monoshock rear suspension was a development of that used on the 1983 GPz1100, as were the anti-dive AVDS- (Automatic Variable Damping System) equipped ▶

RIGHT: The full fairing was another of the Kawasaki's pioneering features which, along with the smaller 16in front wheel, contributed to its slippery aerodynamics. KAWASAKI

RIGHT: Although its compact 908cc four wasn't as powerful as Kawasaki's own 120bhp GPz1100, improved aerodynamics and lighter weight meant it was faster. KAWASAKI

front forks and cast aluminium six-spoke wheels, which were partly chosen to maintain the GPz family 'look' (although the new Ninja did feature a then fashionable 16in front 'hoop' rather than the 1100's 18-incher).

As for the name, although Ninja is a Japanese term, it took an American – Kawasaki USA's director of marketing Mike Vaughan – to persuade the factory to adopt it. "In 1979, they showed us the first GPzs, and I suggested then that we call them 'Ninja'," he later said in an interview with American magazine *Dealernews*. "The Japanese blew it off, and frankly my colleagues weren't crazy about it, either. So, the name was retired to a folder until the GPz900R was revealed. We probably saw the first examples of the bike in late '82. It seemed to me that this really was the Ninja, and I began campaigning for the adoption of the name.

"At about the same time, we switched advertising agencies," Vaughan continued. The old agency, which had held the account for a number of years, was on my side with regard to the name. But the new agency, wanting to establish their 'creds', proposed calling it the 'Panther'."

Vaughan gradually won over his US colleagues, but Kawasaki Japan argued that the Ninjas were outlaws and that the name would therefore be shameful. "I tried to convince them that, because the Ninja concept was unknown to most Americans, the name's image would

be whatever we made it," Vaughan added.

Even so, right up to the GPz900R's launch, Vaughan was sure he'd lost the argument until he got a call one day to say that Kawasaki Japan had finally agreed to call the bike Ninja after a colleague of Vaughan's, Jet Johnson, had successfully lobbied the Kawasaki president.

But the GPz900R Ninja's legendary status was truly earned after it was launched and by the achievements it made afterwards.

Unveiled to the public at the Paris Show in France in the autumn of 1983, the new Kawasaki then had its press riding launch at Laguna Seca raceway in California, USA, in December before going on sale in early 1984. From the outset it was

> ## 66 *Motorcycling had entered a new age* 99

ABOVE: Tom Cruise with his GPz900R in *Top Gun: Maverick*. It was first seen in the first *Top Gun* movie in 1986.
PARAMOUNT PICTURES

clear motorcycling had entered a new age.

At that Paris unveiling, although the GPz900R's claimed peak power figure of 113bhp was actually five LESS than Kawasaki's comparatively old-fashioned, air-cooled GPz1100, its compact, integrated, lightweight layout prompted its maker to describe it as 'having the performance of an 1100 and the agility of a 750'. Kawasaki also claimed its newcomer was the first superbike capable of 150mph, partly due to its aerodynamic fairing, so setting a benchmark that took its rivals years to beat.

While at the world press launch in California, Kawasaki also took the unprecedented move of hiring leading US drag racer Jay 'Pee Wee' Gleason to demonstrate the GPz900R's standing quarter-mile acceleration prowess. He promptly set an elapsed time of 10.55 seconds – a full two seconds faster than its Z1 predecessor – and the world sat up and took notice.

Nor was the new Ninja a one trick, straight-line pony. Around Laguna's sweeping, high-speed turns, the new Kawasak would easily stay with, and invariably out brake and out turn, both the GPz1100 and 750 Turbo that it was launched alongside.

Other records and 'claims to fame' quickly followed. The following May the GPz900R blitzed the 751-1500cc Production TT with Geoff Johnson leading a one-two ahead of Howard Selby. Numerous magazine group tests declared the Kawasaki the new class king around the same time and by August, the Ninja was UK motorcycling's hottest ticket, with lines of red Kawasakis queuing up outside dealers for their

LEFT: Overall, the new Ninja, as it was first called in the USA, became so iconic it even featured in Tom Cruise's blockbuster movie *Top Gun*.
KAWASAKI

ABOVE: Other pioneering features included its AVDS anti-dive forks. KAWASAKI

B-plate release. At year's end, the GPz900R was, almost inevitably, voted *MCN* Machine of the Year.

But the GPz900R's biggest claim to fame was that it reigned supreme for years to come and inspired a whole new class of liquid-cooled, 16 valve, transverse four superbikes in the wake of its success.

When, two years later, *Top Gun* became *the* summer blockbuster movie, it was almost inevitable that the Ninja would be chosen as the bike its motorcycle-mad star, Tom Cruise, would ride.

When updated by the larger, more powerful GPZ1000RX in 1986, then the 137bhp ZX-10 two years after that, the GPz900R remained better than and even outlived both, surviving in Kawasaki's UK range until 1993, with its engine architecture then forming the basis of further world-beaters such as the ZZ-R1100. In 1990 the GPz900R was updated once again, with its front wheel growing from 16 to 17ins to adhere to the then class standard, with it receiving beefier forks and better brakes, too.

In its twilight years, the GPz900R may have come to be regarded more as a budget sports tourer than as the giant-killing superbike it was originally but that shouldn't dent its memory. When the GPz900R was finally replaced in the UK by the 1994 ZX-9R, it was no surprise that it, too, was a 900 Ninja – its legend had been fully cemented by then, after all.

And when the GPz900R finally went out of production after a full 19 years, an astonishing over

RIGHT: It also proved so popular it was repeatedly updated, outlived not one but two of its intended successors, and ultimately remained in production for 19 years. KAWASAKI

77,000 had been built, which is also partly why the Ninja is not quite the collectable classic its achievements probably deserve – there's simply too many of them to be considered special.

With hindsight, the Ninja 900 may be more of a sports tourer than a pure sporting superbike (although, at the time, it was as extreme as Japanese bikes got). Also, TT exploits aside, it was no real race winner, mostly due to it not fitting in with the then 750cc superbike racing rules. Even so, the GPz900R is still every bit as deserving as any other to be included here.

The GPz900R's legacy is probably two-fold: its faired, compact, liquid-cooled, 16v, transverse four with monoshock suspension layout was truly pioneering and spawned the

template for all Japanese superbikes for the next 30 years.

While, as the first Ninja, the name that has been applied to pretty much all Kawasaki sports bikes since, the GPz900R is responsible for not just one, but a whole dynasty of superbikes. A junior version, the GPZ600R, followed later that year and became the catalyst for a 600cc 'supersports' class which would be best sellers for the next two decades. In the US Ninja was also applied to the ZZ-R1100, ZX-7R, and others. While in the UK, 'Ninja' came to be used on the GPz9's successor, the ZX-9R Ninja, then the ZX-6R and ZX-12R, right up to the latest ZX-4R.

For that, and for so much more, the GPz900R is a legend. World records, racing success, mass popularity and Hollywood glamour – the first Ninja had it all. ■

1985 SUZUKI

The first true superbike 'racer replica' which kickstarted a Suzuki dynasty

There is no better known or arguably more successful modern superbike family than that of Suzuki's GSX-R. Whether in 600, 1000 or original 750cc guise, the 'Gixxer' has done it all: won racing championships, become the go-to bike for street loons, and sold over a million all told.

That success is largely down to the impact of the original, the GSX-R750F. Unveiled at the Cologne Show in Germany in the autumn 1984, it caused an immediate sensation. With clip-ons, full race fairing, endurance bike-style twin headlights and a pioneeringly lightweight aluminium chassis, no sports bike had ever looked so focused. And, with a dry weight of just 176kg (33kg less than Yamaha's new FZ750 of the same year) and a revvy, class-leading 100bhp, it promised the performance to back up that style, too.

It delivered exactly that. In 1985's new *MCN* Streetbike production race series GSX-Rs won nine of the 11 races (FZ750s won the other two) with ultimate series winner Mick Grant sweeping the first four. And

when the bigger GSX-R1100 arrived in 1986 to a similar impact, a dynasty was begun which remains to this day. The racer replica was here to stay.

The GSX-R was inspired by Suzuki's long racing history, starting with 50 and 125cc 1960s two-strokes leading to the RG500 of Barry Sheene in the 1970s, which all promoted Suzuki's then road-going GT strokers. Yet as the decade's end came near, it was clear that a different approach was now needed.

With the GTs set to be replaced by a new breed of four strokes, starting with the 1976 GS750, then the GS1000 and GSX1100, Suzuki's racing programme began to be more four-stroke orientated as well.

The works XR69 came first, an F1 machine using a tuned GS1000 engine in a tubular steel chassis which won the prestigious 1980

ABOVE: The original GSX-R750 may not have been the first racer replica, but it was the one that kicked off the popularity of the breed, inspiring a whole new GSXR dynasty. SUZUKI

LEFT: The all-new, oil-cooled engine was another key element that would remain a GSX-R 'signature' for years to come. SUZUKI

GSX-R750F

Suzuka 8 Hours endurance race. That was followed by the 1982 XR41 with a lighter, box-section aluminium frame and monoshock rear suspension. And *that* bike's success convinced Suzuki that lightweight aluminium frames were fundamental to its sporting future, so prompting the 1983 RG250 two-stroke followed by the first GSX-R (with the 'R' standing for 'race-replica GSX') – the 1984 four-cylinder, Japan-only GSX-R400.

Of course, that was just the start. For its bigger 'world market' GSX-R, Suzuki had even bolder ambitions. Until then, the company had soldiered on with its air cooled, two-valve GSs and four-valve GSXs, while Honda had stolen a march with its first liquid-cooled V4s. Kawasaki's new GPz900R was also in the works around the same time.

So, with the American Motorcyclist Association (AMA) in 1983 reducing its Superbike capacity limit to 750cc, Suzuki decided its forthcoming GSX-R750 would leapfrog them all. The project was led by ex-racer Etsuo Yokouchi, who was determined to bring the lightness and purity of a racer to the street; the XR41 racer was its catalyst and ultra lightness became the overall goal.

The GSX-R400 had already shown that a 15-20% weight reduction was possible. "I felt we should be able to do the same with a 750," Yokouchi said later. He then set the goals for the GSX-R750: peak power of 100bhp, a top speed of 146mph, and dry weight of just 176kg.

Part of the process saw Yokouchi's team disassemble a 1983 GSX750 and mark every component blue or red – blue for those with no reliability issues, red if they wore quickly. "When we brought all the parts together, they were almost all blue!" Yokouchi remembered. "We were building the bike too well, too conservative!"

Water-cooling wasn't an option due to the added weight as casting techniques weren't yet optimised, so Yokouchi and engine group leader Tatsunobu Fujii came up with an enhanced air/oil-cooling system, the Suzuki Advanced Cooling System (SACS), which allowed the new engine to keep cool and so achieve 100bhp. The new cooling system helped boost power by allowing smaller, lighter pistons and higher compression. Flat-slide carburettors, until then the preserve of motocrossers, were also used to improve throttle response and fuel atomisation. And the GSX-R also featured the Twin Swirl Combustion Chamber (TSCC) head design as introduced on the 1980 GSX1100. The result not only attained the target of 100bhp, achieved at 10,500rpm, it set a new class standard.

Elsewhere, the focus was primarily on lightness. The GSX-R's pistons were lighter by 10%, con-rods by ▶

SPECIFICATIONS

Price new	£3,499
Engine	748cc oil-cooled DOHC transverse four
Power	100bhp @ 10,500rpm
Torque	54lb-ft @ 10,000rpm
Frame	Box-section aluminium cradle
Suspension	41mm telescopic forks (F), monoshock (R)
Brakes	2 x 300mm discs (F), 220mm disc (R)
Tyres	110/80 x 18 (F), 140/70 x 18 (R)
Dry weight	176kg
Top speed	147mph

It was inspired by Suzuki's factory F1 and endurance racers, the XR41 and XR69, with both emphasising lightweight and revvy, tuned engines. SUZUKI

25%, its crankshaft by nearly 20%, a pioneering cast magnesium cylinder head by 22%, and its cylinder block by another 17%.

Meanwhile, the chassis team, led by Hiroshi Fujiwara, worked to create a stronger version of the GSX-R400's frame and the result, at just over 8kg, weighed less than half that of the previous GS's steel version.

Other chassis parts were similarly light. The GSX-R's thin-wall 41mm forks weighed no more than the spindlier 37mm tubes of the GS. New-generation 'Full-Floater' rear suspension was mated to a box-section aluminium swingarm, lightweight 18in wheels used hollow axles and were stopped by drilled 300mm discs, and the triple clamps were alloy, too.

> ## 66 *Suddenly, starting grids were full of GSX-Rs* 99

At 176kg dry, the result was far lighter than any rival (as well as being lighter than the new Yamaha FZ750, the GSX-R was nearly a full 45kg lighter than Honda's VF750F). Nor did it end there: the slab-sided (hence 'Slabby' nickname) bodywork mimicked the XR41 wherever possible. "We wanted a racebike look," said styling chief Tetsumi Ishii. The dash mimicked the racer too, comprising just a white-faced speedo and tacho (plus required fuel gauge on domestic variants) mounted in foam.

The finished production machine was unveiled at the Cologne Show in October 1984. It caused an immediate sensation and suddenly production racing grids were full of GSX-Rs. The new Suzuki dominated 1985's inaugural *MCN* Superstock British Championship and took the first four places in that year's Production TT.

American *Cycle World* magazine said in May of 1985: "For sheer performance, the GSX-R can't be beaten. It's quicker and faster than the Yamaha FZ750 due to its light weight and high power. The Suzuki feels like a race bike on which someone has done an exceptionally thorough job of conversion, making it into a street bike by adding lights, an effective muffler, and some padding to the seat."

That year Trevor Nation rode his Metzeler production championship GSX-R750 1,000 miles to Portugal to compete in the Formula One race in Vila Real. He said later: "The GSX-R made a huge impact on me. It did 147mph, which was miles quicker than any production bike I'd ridden before, and I loved the way you felt a part of the bike, too. From a mechanical point of view, it was a true Suzuki of that time with nothing unnecessary on it. It was beautiful.

"With a gap in my domestic season, I was looking for excuses to keep riding it, so I thought 'let's have a go in the Formula One road race at Vila Real, in Portugal'. Preparation was limited. I looked at the map and sort of aimed for Biarritz, where I stopped and camped by the roadside. I had my Oxford tank bag and some other soft luggage, and a Michelin slick on the back for the race.

"After the race, [he finished down the field after a nut came off the gear lever pivot shaft] I put my road tyres back on and rode to Barcelona for the next round, then rode home again. What a great bike!"

Crucially, though (and just as significantly) again that was also just the start. The GSX-R750F's success led to a GSX-R1100 in 1986, and their combined success spawned a whole family of GSX-Rs that live on as Suzuki's sportsters.

A year after the game-changing GSX-R750F, Suzuki followed it up with a bigger, more powerful GSX-R1100 and, with 125bhp, the lightest weight in the class and pure racer styling, the big 'Gixxer' eleven instantly gained a reputation as the fastest and fiercest hyperbike around.

To produce it, the 750's oil-cooled engine was bored and stroked to 1052cc, boosting not just power, but torque. That added grunt allowed the '11' just five instead of the 750's six gears, with a fatter-still rear tyre. While, to maintain stability, the wheelbase was also significantly longer.

There were other changes, too. The 1100's box-section aluminium frame had broader, stronger sections, its steering geometry was slightly slower, its riding position slightly roomier, and the 1100 was heavier, too. All of that made the

1100 more stable, solid and flexible than the 750 – a big pussycat, providing you were careful with your right wrist.

And although the 'eleven' couldn't quite match the 750's success, arriving later and gaining less publicity, it quickly carved a place in motorcycling's hierarchy as the biggest, baddest and most bristly sports bike around, while both bikes created a GSX-R dynasty – and a rivalry with Yamaha's FZRs – which would largely define superbikes for the next decade.

Those '80s GSX-Rs also saw rapid evolution, with some big changes. The 1985 GSX-R750F changed into the 1986 G with a longer swing arm. The 1987 GSX-R1100H, meanwhile, gained new paint and front mudguard. Then 1988 saw the GSX-R750J 'Slingshot', its nickname derived from its new 36mm constant-velocity semi-flat slide carbs, but in truth, pretty much the whole bike was new with a revised, short-stroke motor boosting bhp from 100 to 112, uprated suspension and new four-pot brakes, new, smaller 17in wheels, more compact dimensions and smoother styling, although, on the down side it was heavier, too.

1990 saw the GSX-R750L, distinguished by the first use of inverted forks on a large capacity Japanese machine, a return to the long-stroke motor plus other modifications which saw power up to 115bhp at 11,000rpm and weight back down to 193kg.

1992 saw the GSX-R750WN, which was the next big change when an all-new liquid-cooled engine (in place of oil cooling) debuted, resulting in a more compact design and power up again to 118bhp. And there were later changes, too, both to the 750 and its 1100c bigger brother.

By then, however, although the Gixxer was by then firmly established as the hooligan superbike for the street, it was also falling behind a new generation of lightweight, beam-framed rivals such as Honda's FireBlade, Kawasaki's ZXR750J and Yamaha's latest YZF750R which would ultimately lead to Suzuki creating its own with the all-new, Moto GP-inspired, beam-framed GSX-R750WT in 1997 (see p76).

But, for the most part, that didn't matter. The original GSX-R750F in 1985 had been truly revolutionary, redefining what a superbike could be, creating a new Suzuki dynasty and inspiring a new breed of racer replicas.

The GSX-R's raw performance also appealed to hooligans who, having crashed their 'Gixxers', binned their fairings and added wheelie-friendly motocross handlebars, creating the 'streetfighter'.

"For me GSX-R is a symbol of what being an engineer is all about," Chiaki Hirata, who worked on the engine, remembered on the GSX-R's 30th anniversary. "With this motorcycle Suzuki achieved the impossible and it connected the entire team and company together solidly. The GSX-R definitely made Suzuki a stronger company."

It also made a motorcycling legend. As one journalist at the time reported: "From now we'll be talking about sports bikes before the GSX-R, and those after…"

No superbike has a greater legacy than that. Fans of the modern racer replicas, sporting Suzukis, streetracers and more owe an awful lot to the original GSX-R. ■

BELOW: The GSX-R also underlined its significance by becoming an instant winner on track in production racing, first in the *MCN* Streetbike series, then, here with American racer Kevin Schwantz. SUZUKI

1985 YAMAHA FZ750

The five-valve pioneer that paved the way for all FZRs to come

The Suzuki GSX-R750 wasn't the only game-changing Japanese 750 superbike launched in 1985. Yamaha, by then virtually fully committed to the four-stroke engine after its two-stroke origins and long history, launched its first truly modern, liquid cooled, 750cc, transverse four superbike. The resulting FZ750 was also pioneering

LEFT: The first to be produced under Yamaha's integrated 'Genesis' concept, it featured an all-new five-valve engine and wraparound box section steel frame. YAMAHA

SPECIFICATIONS

Price new	£3,299
Engine	749cc liquid-cooled DOHC transverse four
Power	105bhp @ 10,500rpm
Torque	60lb-ft @ 8,000rpm
Frame	Box-section steel perimeter
Suspension	Telescopic forks (F), monoshock (R)
Brakes	2 x 270mm discs (F), 270mm disc (R)
Tyres	120/80 x 16 (F), 130/80 x 18 (R)
Dry weight	209kg
Top speed	145mph

as it introduced revolutionary five-valve heads and a new concept where engine and chassis were designed to work together for optimum performance that Yamaha called 'Genesis'. Both were to remain keystones for the manufacturer's superbike development over the next two decades.

In a multivalve four-stroke engine, one of the keys to maximum rpm – and thus power – is valve area and therefore its ability to flow fuel. This is why the two-valve engine of the CB750 was superseded by the four-valve of the later CB750F. In a similar way, Suzuki progressed from the two-valve GS1000E to the four-valve GSX1100.

For its challenge to the superbike establishment, however, which would also succeed its ageing, obsolete, air-cooled XJ series, Yamaha in the early 1980s shifted to

BELOW: The FZ750 was not only a monumental advance over previous Yamaha superbikes, it helped set the template for other manufacturers, too. YAMAHA

liquid-cooling and began exploring other valve arrangements including even six and seven valve heads, and new, novel downdraught induction, whereby fuel mixture had a shorter, faster route into the combustion chamber via a combination of revised engine layouts and carburettor positioning.

The arrangement Yamaha settled on for the FZ was a double overhead cam head with five valves per cylinder, and downdraught carburettors achieved by inclining the cylinder block at a radical 45°.

By using three intake valves and two exhaust valves per cylinder, it allowed both excellent volumetric efficiency and high rpm. Downdraft carburetors were adopted for improved gas flow, but Yamaha largely avoided the problem of having the airbox above the engine (where the fuel tank would normally be) by inclining the cylinders, building the tank lower and using an electric fuel pump to take fuel to the carburetors. A deeper fuel tank also gave a small advantage as it centralised weight and moved the centre of gravity lower.

All of this also necessarily required the new bike's chassis to be developed in tandem with the engine as opposed to the motor being designed first and the chassis then forced to fit around it as had been common practice at the time. Accordingly, the FZ's designers integrated the whole package and named it the 'Genesis' concept. The process also promoted the use of a perimeter or beam frame as opposed to a spine or cradle frame as also commonly used before.

> ## " At IFMA, the FZ was the talk of the show "

Thus, the FZ was given a perimeter type box-section steel frame designed in tandem with the engine, which was an evolution of the 'Lateral Frame Concept' that debuted on 1983's FJ1100. When this design was further advanced by using more lightweight aluminium beams instead of box-section steel tubes on the succeeding 1987 FZR1000R – a design which Yamaha called 'Deltabox' – it would remain Yamaha's 'go to' superbike layout for the next 30 years.

The FZ was then all rounded off with the latest monoshock rear suspension, a fashionable 16in front wheel for nimble steering and a stylish, frame-mounted half-fairing which Yamaha purposely chose both to be different from the trend for 'racer replicas' but also to draw the eye to its pioneering inclined engine block. In 1985, the FZ750 may have been only four years on from Yamaha's old XS1100, but in terms of modernity, it seemed like 40.

In September 1984 at IFMA, the world's largest motorcycle fair, held that year in Cologne in then West Germany, the FZ750 was the talk of the show.

The trouble was, it wasn't the only one – there was also Suzuki's all-new, racier GSX-R750 to contend with. Initially, the FZ came out on top. Magazine tests praised the Yamaha for its balance of power, handling, and comfort, making it suitable for both street and track use, while many also rated the FZ slightly ahead of the GSX-R as an all-rounder, the UK's *Bike* magazine among them. The Yamaha's 105bhp was also slightly better and far more

FZ750

flexible than the oil-cooled four of the peaky, 100bhp Suzuki.

"In almost every respect the bike's a detuned racer," reported *Which Bike?* magazine in February 1985. "But, like the RD500LC, the quality of the engine and running gear is such that it offers a refined package for the road."

On track, however, especially in the new *MCN* Streetbike racing series, the lighter, more focused GSX-R had the FZ beat.

History tells us that Suzuki's GSX-R750 made a bigger impact, dominating that year's *MCN* racing series and igniting a new era of 'racer replicas' and that, as a result, the FZ750 never quite sold in the numbers it deserved – nor that Yamaha had hoped for.

But the FZ ran it closer than most remember, was the GSX-R's main rival on track (winning two of the ten *MCN* rounds), was better, more versatile on the road and, with its five valves and pioneering frame technology, was arguably an even more significant technological catalyst for the superbikes that were yet to come.

The FZ's perceived failure also emboldened Yamaha to go further still, leading to the racier, 999cc FZR1000R in 1987, which usurped Suzuki's GSX-R1100, introduced the aluminium Deltabox frame, and is regarded as the finest superbike of the era.

Yamaha's pioneering five-valve technology lived on, leading to 1989's OW01 and game-changing 1998 R1, before eventually being dropped due to other advances in the late noughties.

So, while the first Gixxer invented the 'racer replica' and was the winner on track, the core concepts of the FZ were arguably just as significant. The FZ750 itself was undoubtedly the first of Yamaha's great modern superbikes and a hugely significant catalyst for all that was to follow. ■

ABOVE: Unfortunately, the FZ was also launched around the same time as Suzuki's more extreme GSX-R750, so wasn't the success hoped for. YAMAHA

BELOW: Other pioneering elements included downdraught carburettors, which dictated the angle of the cylinder block be inclined forwards by 45°. YAMAHA

1987 YAMAHA FZR1000

Yamaha's first aluminium-framed, litre-class superbike

After Kawasaki set the ball rolling for fine-handling sports bikes with the integrated design of its GPZ900R Ninja in 1984, Suzuki introduced the lightweight, no compromise 'race replica' with its first GSX-R750 the following year, rivals Yamaha were the next Japanese brand to truly move sports bikes forward with its FZR1000R of 1987.

That first 'big' FZR, often referred to as the 'Genesis', is regarded as one of finest litre-class sports motorcycles of the late 1980s. Unusually, though, this wasn't for its prodigious power (although with 125bhp it had plenty) but for its revolutionary frame and all-round brilliant handling.

SPECIFICATIONS

Price new	£4,969
Engine	989cc liquid-cooled DOHC transverse four
Power	125bhp @ 10,000rpm
Torque	75lb-ft @ 8,500rpm
Frame	Aluminium twin spar
Suspension	41mm telescopic forks (F), monoshock (R)
Brakes	2 x 317mm discs (F), 264mm disc (R)
Tyres	120/70 x 17 (F), 160/60 x 18 (R)
Dry weight	204kg
Top speed	158mph

Unveiled at the Cologne Show in 1986, the FZR1000 combined Yamaha's recent advances in engine and chassis design in one thoroughly developed 989cc package. This was the heart of Yamaha's Genesis ideology where its advanced multi-valve engines and perimeter chassis were designed to function together to provide optimum power and handling.

The FZR's four-cylinder engine was developed from that of Yamaha's 1985 FZ750, complete with unique five valves and a cylinder block inclined forwards by 35°– but with its capacity enlarged to 989cc. Far more revolutionary, though, was the combination of this engine with a pioneering twin spar aluminium frame which Yamaha called 'Deltabox'. The design, whereby beefy, rigid but lightweight aluminium beams linked the headstock and swingarm pivot virtually in a straight line with the engine suspended within, had been pioneered in 500 GP racing.

Yamaha had actually debuted the technology a year earlier on its Japan-only FZR400 Genesis, but the 1987 1000 was the first time it had been used on a large capacity, production road machine.

The result, with quality but largely conventional suspension, 17in front and 18in rear wheels, big, powerful 320mm floating disc brakes and all-enveloping bodywork, was the most complete and integrated litre-class sportsbike yet built. Yamaha called it the 'Ultimate Road Machine' and they weren't wrong. On the street, the new FZR1000 was more controlled and effective than Suzuki's comparatively cumbersome and crude GSX-R1100. While on track, although at 1000cc the FZR was ineligible for the new 750cc Superbike racing class, the new Yamaha cleaned up in national 1300cc production racing and won the Castrol Six Hour in Australia and Production TT on the Isle of Man.

But if the aluminium twin spar 'revolution' began with the 1987

ABOVE: After the disappointment of the FZ750, the racier, larger FZR1000R, complete with Yamaha's first aluminium Deltabox frame proved a huge success. YAMAHA

'Genesis', there was better still to come with the first significantly updated FZR1000 EXUP in 1989 which overnight became the king superbike of the early 1990s.

EXUP was Yamaha's acronym for its Exhaust Ultimate Power Valve, a four-stroke version of the YPVS (Yamaha Power Valve System) pioneered on Yamaha's two-strokes, such as the 1983 RD350, which changed the exhaust tuning in response to changes in engine rpm and thus allowed impressive peak power while maintaining strong midrange performance.

That was just the beginning: the updated EXUP's five-valve four went from 989 to 1002cc but was smaller and more compact overall due to a revised cylinder angle. Bigger carburettors further boosted performance, and the crank was strengthened to suit.

Chassis-wise, the new Deltabox II frame was shorter and more compact to take advantage of the revised engine dimensions, there were beefier forks and discs, the 17/18in wheel combination was replaced by 17s front and rear and, although the

EXUP's steering geometry wasn't as sharp, the new bike compensated by having a shorter wheelbase and slightly lower stance.

The end result, in even sleeker bodywork, not only went better, stopped better and handled better – as the world's press discovered when it was launched at Laguna Seca, California, in late October 1988 – it also felt more integrated and looked better. In short, the 1989 EXUP was not only the new superbike 'standard' but was the 'pin-up' 1000cc Japanese superbike into the 1990s.

ABOVE: Powerful, fine handling (due to the Genesis concept and frame) and striking looking, the FZR quickly proved to be the 1000cc superbike to beat. YAMAHA

"The FZR1000EXUP is the fastest, big-bore street bike ever made in Japan," stated *American Motorcyclist* magazine in May 1989.

It was all enough for the 1989 bike to be crowned 'Bike of the Decade' by some critics leaving, you would think, nowhere for any improved version to go. But the 1991 RU achieved just that. That year, the EXUP was honed even further with new inverted front forks and sharper styling with a new, single headlight front cowling to become the FZR1000RU.

Those improvements may seem minor, but bear in mind the brilliant base bike it was built on. The 1987 999cc Genesis had redefined litre-class superbikes by being the first fully integrated design complete with a five-valve head, 135bhp and GP-alike, aluminium twin spar Deltabox frame. The succeeding EXUP in 1989 added power-boosting electronic exhaust valves which, along with three extra cc, boosted power to 145bhp while gaining a revised, more rigid Deltabox II frame with sharper steering and better-looking bodywork. The RU went one further yet again due to improved suspension and styling.

Sure, its reign, due to the imminent 1992 Fireblade, was short, while a further, final 'Foxeye' facelift in 1994 was by then largely irrelevant, but in 1991 the FZR1000RU EXUP was as good as superbikes got.

"This is a sportbike like no other," claimed the US's *Cycle World*, in April 1991. "It's one that leaves even inveterate speed junkies slack-jawed and searching for superlatives. For the past four years, the FZR 1000 has defined the cutting edge of large displacement sportbikes. The edge just got sharper."

But now the Fireblade was just around the corner… ■

LEFT: In this form, and with even better styling, the EXUP as it became known, was the new superbike king. YAMAHA

BELOW: In 1989, the big FZR was uprated again, with an improved Deltabox II frame and the addition of Yamaha's new EXUP exhaust valve. YAMAHA

1987 HONDA RC30

The first true 'homologation special' superbike which dominated racing for years

The RC30 isn't just one of the most revered superbikes of the 1980s – it's one of the greatest road motorcycles of all time.

One of the first 'homologation special' road-legal production racers, the RC30, also known as the VFR750R, was created to win in a new series of 750cc production-based racing formulas introduced in the late 1980s and, by doing so, publicise and promote the more mainstream V4 roadsters Honda was then committed to. The RC30's success, was unprecedented and it became the go-to production racer for the best part of a decade. It was successful over a broad range of bike sport – world superbikes, endurance, TT racing and more – that no bike has since come close and, today, as a result, the RC30 enjoys unmatched stature as one of the most collectable superbikes of modern times.

By 1984, Honda was beginning to take serious interest in endurance racing as well as the blossoming British TTF1 series, and its RS750R works racer, based on the VF750F, was the result. That then developed into the RVF750R, which Wayne Gardner rode to victory in the 1985 Suzuka 8 Hours race and world endurance championship.

However, sales of Honda's then road-going V4s remained slow, so Honda then came up with the first VFR750F with a new, lighter engine with a 180° crankshaft and box-section aluminum frame.

At the same time, the world production racing landscape was about to change fundamentally, too. Former US racer Steve McLaughlin proposed a new international 750cc four-stroke road bike series called World Superbikes (WSB). Compared

<table>
<tr><td colspan="2">SPECIFICATIONS</td></tr>
<tr><td>Price new</td><td>£8,499</td></tr>
<tr><td>Engine</td><td>748cc liquid-cooled DOHC 90° V4</td></tr>
<tr><td>Power</td><td>118bhp @ 11,000rpm</td></tr>
<tr><td>Torque</td><td>53lb-ft @ 10,500rpm</td></tr>
<tr><td>Frame</td><td>Aluminium twin spar</td></tr>
<tr><td>Suspension</td><td>43mm telescopic forks (F), monoshock (R)</td></tr>
<tr><td>Brakes</td><td>2 x 310mm discs (F), 220mm disc (R)</td></tr>
<tr><td>Tyres</td><td>120/70 x 17 (F), 170/60 x 18 (R)</td></tr>
<tr><td>Dry weight</td><td>185kg</td></tr>
<tr><td>Top speed</td><td>153mph</td></tr>
</table>

ABOVE: Although at 112bhp it was not outrageously fast, the RC30 handled superbly, was tunable and durable, too. It looked fantastic. HONDA

LEFT: The RC30 was Honda's bespoke, homologation-special, road legal superbike aimed at the new formula of 750cc production racing. HONDA

ABOVE: A V4 intended to popularise Honda's more mainstream V4s, the RC30 (or VFR750R) also boasted an aluminium twin spar frame, quick-release wheels, and more. HONDA

BELOW: It was all enough to win not only the World Superbike crown first time out, but the second, plus F1, world endurance and TT races. HONDA

to F1, WSB was production based and more restrictive, requiring unchanged chassis, engine casings, carbs and more. The previously all-conquering RVF750R was no longer eligible, Honda racing boss Michihiko Aika backed the idea, seeing its potential to promote its 750, and Honda Racing Corporation (HRC) began developing a new limited edition V4 road bike that could win it. That bike would be the 1988 VFR750R (RC30).

In 1987 a prototype called the 6X raced at Suzuka and Isle of Man TT. In July that year, Honda finally officially announced that they had a new homologation machine for the forthcoming World Superbike Championship. The VFR750R's official launch took place towards the end of the year at a wet Suzuka when it was clear that any thought that it was simply a 'souped up' VFR750F was immediately scotched. Soon after, it entered limited production and the rest, as they say, is history. In 1988 the RC30 promptly won the inaugural

Superbike World Championship before going on to win a long list of national and international championships over the next six years. No production racer since has come close.

Although a production, road-legal superbike, and ostensibly technically based on the latest VFR750F, the resemblance was superficial with every RC30 instead built by a small team of dedicated technicians at HRC.

Before 1988, other bikes had full fairings, aluminium beam frames, fully adjustable suspension, dinner-plate disc brakes, and even single-sided swingarms. The RC30 was the first to combine them all. It was the summation of a century's worth of frame, tyre, brake and steering geometry development in one bike, and the first to get them all absolutely right.

Although sharing the same bore and stroke as the F, the R's V4 was fundamentally different, with a 360° firing order, gear-driven cams, titanium con rods and valves, a slipper clutch, and a close-ratio, race-type gearbox.

Camshafts ran in needle-roller and roller bearings, acting directly on the valve stems; the elimination of rocker arms allowing for a more compact cylinder-head casting. No oil cooler was fitted, instead oil temperature was reduced by running engine coolant through a small circular radiator mounted adjacent to the oil filter. Two large radiators (one with fan assistance) carried the engine

> *At the first WSB race the RC30 took pole*

coolant. The result was a fast, but equally important, flexible and reliable 118bhp with a rich, droning exhaust note.

Chassis-wise, the RC30 was based on the aluminum twin-spar RVF750 with what Honda called the 'Diamond Frame Concept' which used the engine as a stressed member. The RVF had made good use of the Elf-patented single-sided swinging arm with the wheel retained by a single nut which allowed rapid wheel changes where the rear sprocket and chain remained in place, and the RC30 retained this feature. (Honda paid royalties to the French fuel company for each item produced.) There was also fully adjustable Showa suspension, quick-release wheel clamps and brake pads, and a 'Pro Squat Rear Brake Linkage' to reduce the rear wheel hopping when braking. While the RC30's ultra clean racing bodywork included a single seat and twin headlamps, again for world endurance.

The result looked exquisite, handled beautifully, was fast, light, compact, durable and beautifully made. It went on sale in Japan in late 1987, before being exported globally in spring 1988.

Many privateers bought RC30s to race straight from the crate. An extensive race kit was made available to teams to prepare the road-based bike ready for the track, while full-factory 'NL0' versions were official entries in road racing, and world endurance, including the Suzuka 8 Hours.

At the first WSB race in May it took pole position, while Fred Merkel rode one to both that and the following year's championship. Carl Fogarty did a similar double in a downgraded F1, while at the TT, where the RC30 dominated for a decade, Joey Dunlop won first time out.

Restricted, homologation-only, production ensured the Honda remained rare — especially on the street. A total of 4,782 were built between 1987 and 1990, with just 519 coming to the UK. As such, it was the most desirable Japanese sports machine of its day and remains one of the most exclusive and collectable bikes of the 1980s. ■

1987 DUCATI 851/888

Bordi's masterpiece which prope led Ducati into a new superbike era

Many assume it was the iconic 916 that propelled Ducati into modern times. Others say the popularity of the monster sent the Italian marque into a new era. In truth it was the 'feeder' bike for the 1987 851, later the 888, that was the catalyst for a reborn Ducati.

Before the Bologna brand was bought from the brink of bankruptcy by the Cagiva-owning Castiglioni brothers in 1985, it had a long history of V-twin superbike success dating back to Paul Smart's 1972 Imola 200 winner. By then, however, the classic 'Desmo' air-cooled V-twin, as designed by Fabio Taglioni, was obsolete, while its most modern offering, the belt-drive Pantah, was just 650cc.

But with the Castiglionis craving change and Taglioni semi-retired, his junior protégé, Massimo Bordi, who, for his engineering degree in 1973 had proposed a new four-valve Ducati Desmo, got a golden opportunity.

"When Castiglioni bought Ducati in 1985, he asked me to do something to recapture the technological leadership of Ducati engines," Bordi recalled years later. "My idea was to produce an engine based on the same architecture as the Pantah – a 90° V-twin – but with a totally new concept."

That new concept, designed in conjunction with Gianluigi Mengoli, was not just a four-valve Desmo, but one with liquid-cooling and fuel-injection.

The first result was the 1986 748 IE prototype racer featuring 748cc, four-valves, Desmo heads, and fuel injection on modified Pantah crankcases in a reworked TT1 frame. First raced at the 1986 Bol d'Or by Juan Garriga, Marco Lucchinelli and Virginio Ferrari, it produced 92bhp and impressed before retiring after 15 hours due to a broken conrod bolt.

That evolved into the first 851 prototype of 1987 with redesigned heads, strengthened crankcases and increased capacity resulting in 120bhp, which Lucchinelli rode to victory at Daytona's 1987 Battle of the Twins. Ducati then decided to enter the new World Superbike (WSB) championship the following

LEFT: Race development initially progressed with former GP world champion Marco Lucchinelli before, in 1990, with Frenchman Raymond Roche it won its first crown. DUCATI

BELOW: Ducati's superbike 'revolution' began with the 1987 851 with, at its heart, the new liquid-cooled, four-valve Desmodromic V-twin developed by Massimo Bordi. DUCATI

year, which, being production based, necessitated the 851 going into production. Two versions were offered: the 'Tricolore' 851 Strada, with detuned engine and 16in wheels, of which just 300 were made, plus the 851 Superbike Kit with 17in wheels for racers.

Even then success didn't come quickly. While the racer won first time out at Donington Park with Lucchinelli, financial problems meant Ducati did not enter the final four races in Australia and New Zealand, and Lucchinelli ultimately finished fifth overall behind Merkel's RC30, Pirovano's OW01, and the two Bimotas of Tardozzi and Mertens.

The road bike, meanwhile, had its own problems: without any geometry changes to compensate for the smaller wheels, it was found to have 'dubious' handling.

For 1989, however, the now all-red Strada got 17in wheels and new rider Raymond Roche progressed the racer to third in the championship.

Even though the original 851 had debuted Bordi's new 'Desmoquattro' so revolutionising the Bologna brand, the new four-valve, liquid-cooled, 90° 'L-twin' only truly came 'on song' when updated to 888cc from 1990.

That year saw the release of the 851 SP2 homologation special which had a 2mm larger bore taking capacity to 888cc, Öhlins suspension, fully floating Brembo brakes, 45mm Termignoni exhausts, and was not only a true racer for the road but, in 'Corse' race spec, again in the hands of Roche, won Ducati's first WSB crown starting an era of Ducati superbike dominance continued almost to this day.

The SP2 was succeeded by the 1991 SP3, with louder, higher Termignoni exhausts, black Brembo wheels and higher compression which, with a forced air intake, boosted power to 118bhp and gave Canadian Doug Polen his first WSB crown.

Then, in 1992, both the Strada and new SP4 received a facelift, new dual seat and curved radiator, and was joined by the new 888 Sport Production Special (SPS) with larger, higher lift valves, race cooling and carbon fibre Termignoni exhausts, mirroring the 888 Corse that Polen took to his second title, but with lights and mirrors.

1992 was also the year the 888 helped propel a certain Carl Fogarty towards Ducati superbike stardom. That year, although successful, the Brit was something of a 'journeyman' racer, riding an OW01 for Yamaha in that year's 'greatest ever' TT, and a ZXR750 for Kawasaki France to take the world endurance championship.

But those rides also helped finance his purchase of an 888 Corse for selected rounds of WSB. After two low scoring finishes in Spain, things went from bad to worse at Donington when he crashed out of the first race while leading. But in the second he won, leading to further sponsorship, allowing him to contest the rest of the season. The factory Ducati team duly signed him up for 1993 when, aboard the 888, he finished second behind Scott Russell, before, in 1994, with the new 916, his true golden era began.

"That started everything," 'Foggy' remembered later. "That 888 we bought over the counter was the best bike you could buy to go racing with at the time. The Honda RC30 was three years old by that point. The Yamaha and Kawasaki were good bikes but needed to be converted from road bikes. You bought the Ducati ready to race, so I went for that, and the rest is history."

For its final year in 1993, the road 851 was succeeded by the 888 Strada, which was virtually identical to the 1992 version except for the extra 37cc the SPs had since 1990. The final Sport Production model, meanwhile, the SP5, was based on the SPS but with the SP4's cooling system, Showa forks, and bronze Brembo wheels.

By then, however, a new Ducati superbike – the 916 – was on the horizon. That is another story but without the 851/888, it would never have happened at all… ■

ABOVE: It then evolved into 888 form and as such won two more world superbike titles with Canadian racer Doug Polen. DUCATI

BELOW: Available in homologation 'Superbike' and street trim, the 851 wasn't an immediate success in WSB but was clearly the start of a new era for Ducati. DUCATI

SPECIFICATIONS

Price new	£8,999
Engine	851cc liquid-cooled Desmodromic 90° V-twin
Power	100bhp @ 9,250rpm
Torque	52lb-ft @ 7,250rpm
Frame	Tubular steel trellis
Suspension	42mm telescopic forks (F), monoshock (R)
Brakes	2 x 280mm discs (F), 260mm disc (R)
Tyres	130/60 x 16 (F), 160/60 x 16 (R)
Dry weight	180kg
Top speed	150mph

By the end of the late 1980s, in stark contrast to BMW's current line-up including wacky performance weapons like the M1000RR and six-cylinder mega tourers like the K1600GTL, the German marque instead had probably the most sensible and conservative image of all motorcycle manufacturers and yet it still came up with arguably the most ambitious and radical-looking machine of the era – the K1.

Although not a commercial success, it's fair to say the K1 was, and remains, one of BMW's most significant machines for its role in introducing a raft of new technologies (such as ABS brakes), by reinvigorating its K-series, and for helping form the foundation for the increasingly modern BMW models that followed. Quite simply, without the K1, today's BMW wouldn't be the same...

Although BMW's all-new, liquid-cooled, K-series, first with the four-cylinder 1983 K100RS, then the K100, K75 triple and touring K100RT, had been a sales success, it wasn't as big a success as originally hoped. While initial sales had been good, by 1986 they'd dropped off, exacerbated by the K100RS's 90bhp being quickly overtaken by the new class-leading 108bhp of Kawasaki's 1984 GPz900R then again by Suzuki's 125bhp GSX-R1100. At the same time, BMW also faced growing requests from its more traditional owners for the return of its classic but outdated boxer twins – the very bike the modern K-series had been intended to replace.

The Munich marque needed to act – and it did. First, for 1988, it introduced a new, larger brother to its popular boxer-powered R 80 G/S adventure bike, the R 100GS. Then, at the same, it further appeased boxer fans by reintroducing the R 100RS and R 100 RT.

BMW also knew that a renewed effort was required to establish the K-series as the company's performance and technology motorcycling 'tour-de-force'.

For most motorcycle manufacturers an obvious solution would have been to re-engineer the K100 to produce more power – but BMW wasn't 'most' manufacturers. Back in the late 1980s motorcycles sold in Germany were required to adhere to a maximum power output of 100bhp, a policy BMW supported. So, for any new K-series to have the performance required, another approach was needed.

SPECIFICATIONS

Price new	£8,000
Engine	987cc liquid-cooled DOHC flat four
Power	100bhp @ 8,000rpm
Torque	74lb-ft @ 6,750rpm
Frame	Tubular steel trellis
Suspension	Telescopic forks (F), monoshock (R)
Brakes	2 x 305mm discs (F), 285mm disc (R)
Tyres	120/70 x 17 (F), 160/60 x 18 (R)
Dry weight	235kg
Top speed	150mph

BELOW: No, this is not a screengrab from TV's *Space 1999*, it's a pair of BMW K1s doing what they never did in reality, ride around a racetrack. BMW

1988 BMW K1

How BMW compensated for power with revolutionary aerodynamics

ABOVE: Inside its cockpit, things were far more conventional with one-piece tubular handlebars and an analogue dash borrowed from the K100RS. BMW

RIGHT: The wacky bodywork defined the K1 and was there for much more than styling, being BMW's attempt to counter 100bhp-plus superbike rivals with superior aerodynamics. BMW

BELOW: Although not a sporting or sales success, the K1 put BMW's K-series back on the map and proved significant for the range's ultimate popularity. BMW

Fortunately, one was seemingly available – advanced aerodynamics. BMW had a long history of 'wind cheating' dating back to Ernst Henne's 1930s land speed record streamliners and more recently including its wind tunnel-developed 1976 R100RS. What's more, as recently as 1984, BMW had displayed a 50% scale 'concept' version of a machine called the 'Racer' with radical, all-enclosed bodywork designed by Karl-Heinz Abe.

Although clearly not a viable production machine, this bike provided the inspiration for BMW's new flagship, performance K-series machine. A prototype was green lit by BMW management in June 1986 and given the name K1, in the tradition of BMW's most advanced and pioneering cars, such as the 1978 M1.

And although mechanically based on the K100, the K1 was actually very different. Its 980cc motor received a new four-valve head, lighter pistons and rods, and a completely new Bosch Motronic ignition/fuel injection system to gain not only 10bhp but also an extra 10ft-lb of torque.

Its chassis was significantly uprated, too. While the tubular steel trellis frame looked like the K100's, it was strengthened with revised geometry, including a longer wheelbase, for improved stability. Wheel sizes were changed, there were new, specially developed Marzocchi forks, its brakes were Brembo's latest four-piston caliper type, while the K1 also became the world's first production bike with ABS brakes as standard after BMW's pioneering system was first offered as an option on the K100RS the year before.

Most striking of all was the K1's wind-tunnel developed bodywork. Fully integrated from nose to tail, it comprised seven interlocking glassfibre panels with a matching front mudguard which almost completely covered the wheel, and even a pillion seat cover which was designed to aid airflow.

The result was a sensationally low drag coefficient of 0.36-0.38 (depending on rider size) which helped the K1 to a top speed of 150mph when tested by German magazine *Motorrad,* making it the fastest 100bhp motorcycle of its time.

What's more, in garish red or blue, complete with contrasting yellow graphics, wheels and Paralever rear suspension, when officially unveiled at Cologne in October 1988, the K1 looked sensational.

And yet… it wasn't quite enough. Although it created a furore, achieved its performance goals and introduced a raft of new 'tech', the K1 was still merely brisk rather than rapid. It was also heavy, had a vast turning circle, its enclosing bodywork also proved to be a heat trap, its looks were divisive, and, at £8,000, it was expensive. By the time it was taken out of production in 1993, not quite 7,000 had been sold.

But nor was the K1 a failure. As a range-topping, 'technology spearhead', the K1 fulfilled its role and changed BMW Motorrad's image forever. Its tech and engine were adopted by the 1990 K100RS which became the best-selling K-series so far, leading to the even better 1993 K1100RS. And in 1997, having abandoned the 100bhp limit, that bike was superseded by the all-new 130bhp K1200RS, which kick-started a new era of BMW K 'power'. Without the K1, much of that might not have happened at all and as a result, today, the K1 is rightfully considered a modern classic. ■

1988 KAWASAKI ZXR750

Kawasaki's first world endurance inspired 750cc racer replica...

The launch of the World Superbike championship in 1988 may have been the catalyst for limited edition, 'homologation specials' such as Honda's RC30 and Yamaha's OW01, but there is one Japanese 750 superbike from the era with far more humble origins which became arguably more successful – Kawasaki's ZXR750.

Where the Honda and Yamaha were no expense spared 'exotica' few could afford, Kawasaki did things the other way round – with an affordable, mass-produced sportster that could be converted into a racer. Or, to put it another way: if the expensive, exclusive, RC30 and OW01 were motorcycling royalty, the affordable, mass-market ZXR was the bike for the people.

But the ZXR was no pretender, either – it had genuine pedigree and performance. It was developed from Kawasaki's existing GPX750 with modifications inspired by its prototype ZXR-7 endurance racer (hence the name).

So, it got a new, low slung, twin spar frame, endurance bodywork including 'hoover' air inlet pipes, uprated brakes and suspension and endurance-style paint. The result may have been slightly 'old tech', but it was also one of the best-looking of all 'racer replicas' and, at £5,299, affordable – certainly compared to the £8,499 RC30 and £12,700 OW01.

LEFT: Kawasaki's first true 'racer replica' style superbike was the 1989 ZXR750H1 which proved fine handling, great looking and, importantly, affordable. KAWASAKI

The ZXR went well, too. Its 105bhp was not earth shattering but it was enough for 150mph. It may have been slightly heavy with basic suspension, but it steered and stopped sublimely. And, with great looks and robust build, it proved a sensible superbike buy and instant sales hit.

If Kawasaki's first ZXR750, the H1 of 1989, was an endurance-inspired replica intended for the working man, then its successors, the 1991 ZXR750J1 then the 1993 L1, took things to another level on the road and, in homologation race spec as the ZXR750K and M respectively, on the track, too.

With new, more curvy styling, the J also boasted new inverted forks, a lighter, diamond section beam frame, new short stroke engine and yet still cost just £6,379 (when an RC30 cost £10,000).

Admittedly, its 100bhp peak power was 5bhp down on the H (due mostly to concerns about possible impending power limits), and early examples' rear shocks were rock hard – but it didn't matter: the ZXR-J looked great, had one of the best front ends around (again) and, with race wins across the globe, became THE 'poster bike' 750 of the day.

The ZXR was also a survivor after its peak glory days on track and street were long gone. The 1993 'L' got a ram-air nose and 18 extra bhp, then in 1996 it morphed into the ZX-7R, as which it continued as one of the most recognisable racer replicas of all, right into the new millennium. ∎

BELOW LEFT: The 1991 J1 version proved even more successful and spawned a homologation special which won the Superbike World Championship with Scott Russell. KAWASAKI

SPECIFICATIONS

Price new	£5,299
Engine	749cc liquid-cooled DOHC transverse four
Power	107bhp @ 10,500rpm
Torque	49lb-ft @ 9,000rpm
Frame	Aluminium twin spar
Suspension	43mm telescopic forks (F), monoshock (R)
Brakes	2 x 310mm discs (F), 230mm disc (R)
Tyres	120/70 x 17 (F), 170/60 x 18 (R)
Dry weight	205kg
Top speed	153mph

1992 BIMOTA TESI 1D

The hub-centre steered wonder... that ultimately proved a superbike folly

RIGHT: It was a full eight years in development and the pet project of Bimota's chief engineer Pier Luigi Marconi who first conceived of it at university. BIMOTA

BELOW: In 1992 the world hadn't seen anything quite like the Tesi 1D with, not just a Ducati 851 V-twin engine but also a pioneering hub-centre steered chassis. BIMOTA

When it comes to 'exotica', a term often bandied about to describe expensive, exquisite superbikes whose performance is only bettered by their style and componentry, for much of the 1980s and 1990s, no one did it better than Bimota.

Founded in Rimini in 1973 by Valerio Bianchi, Giuseppe Morri, and Massimo Tamburini (hence BiMoTa), its first bike, the 1975 HB1, was a frame kit for Honda's CB750, its first production bike was 1977's astonishing Suzuki GS750-powered SB2 both leading to Bimota becoming famous for exquisite sportsters based around Japanese engines. Initially, they were tubular steel trellis wrapped around air-cooled fours, then later pioneering aluminium beam frames powered by Yamahas, such as the 1988 FZ750-based YB4ie.

From 1989, now led by Pier Luigi Marconi and with Japanese bikes now commonly having aluminium beam frames of their own, Bimota became even bolder still and the boldest of all is the machine which kicked off this era – the Test 1D.

Unveiled at the Cologne Show in October 1990, the Tesi dated back to the early 1980s when young engineering student Marconi began his degree at Bologna University.

In 1982, he developed a concept foregoing conventional telescopic forks for a front swinging arm with hub-centre steering. After joining Bimota, he built his first running prototype using a Honda VF400 V4 engine, displayed at the 1983 Milan Show as the first 'Tesi' (Italian for 'thesis'). But it wasn't until 1987 that the first production Tesi was scheduled and even then, it got pushed back due to a lack of finance.

When finally unveiled, the Tesi 1D – D designating its 851 powerplant, so also becoming the first Ducati-powered Bimota since 1983's DB1 – caused a sensation. Aside from the hub-centre front end, the liquid-cooled desmo V-twin was state-of-the-art, its 'Omega' frame plates hand-machined aluminium, cycle parts were the best from Marchesini, Brembo and Öhlins, and even the dash was a pioneering LCD digital affair.

It worked pretty well, too. The hub-centre set-up minimised dive and was mostly precise and intuitive; the engine was thunderous and engaging, and the bike's presence was like something from another world.

Trouble was, the steering's rose-joints were reliant on constant maintenance and wore prematurely. The Tesi was also heavy, its dash (and electricals) proved erratic and, worst of all, its £25,000 price was almost triple that of the donor 851. As a result, just 127 were produced from 1990 to 1991, total Bimota production dropped below 500 bikes per year, and the firm's future hung in the balance.

Even if the Tesi 1D promised much yet ended up almost bankrupting Bimota, it was not the end of the story. An improved successor, the Tesi 2D, came out in 2004, followed by the 3D in 2007, while today's Kawasaki-owned Bimota chose the Tesi as the template for its first new bike. Without the Tesi, maybe modern Bimota wouldn't exist at all... ∎

SPECIFICATIONS

Price new	£25,000
Engine	851cc liquid cooled Desmodromic 90° V-twin
Power	103bhp @ 9,500rpm
Torque	61.2lb-ft @ 7,850rpm
Frame	Machined aluminium
Suspension	Hub-centre single shock (F), monoshock (R)
Brakes	2 x 320mm discs (F), 230mm disc (R)
Tyres	120/70 x 17 (F), 180/55 x 17 (R)
Dry weight	188kg
Top speed	155mph

1992 HONDA CBR900RR FIREBLADE

The ultralight 'game changer' that changed superbike design forever

The FireBlade is one of the most famous and successful names in motorcycling, and it's the bike that put Honda back on the sports bike map. With its design focused on being light weight and easy to manage, it set the template for all superbikes that followed.

Not bad for a bike which contained no revolutionary technology, wasn't the fastest or most powerful, was also a Honda which, by 1992, homologation special RC30 aside, hadn't produced a pure, big bore sports bike for a decade, had a name mistranslated from Japanese, or for a project from a first timer with little formal training in bike design...

The 1992 CBR900RR FireBlade project was famously led by Tadao Baba who joined Honda in 1962, worked as a machinist then test rider, before moving into product development. In 1987, he took over leadership of the company's new sports bike project, a key sector then dominated by Yamaha's FZR1000 and Suzuki's GSX-R1100 in which Honda hadn't had a credible contender for nearly a decade.

He later recalled: "It was in 1989, and I was riding with a group of Honda engineers on some competitor machines, a Suzuki GSX-R1100, Yamaha FZR1000, and our own CBR1000F. I was thinking, 'How can these be called sports bikes when they are so very big and heavy?' They didn't deserve the name."

Baba began developing a new sports motorcycle concept with the working title 'Total Control' whereby the overriding principle was to create a larger capacity sports machine that was both fun to ride and easy to control.

"Of course, I was nervous – it was my first project," Baba continued.

LEFT: The first 1992-93 FireBlade was available in a choice of two colour schemes, Honda red/white/blue or this very moody black option. HONDA

"But I was also confident, too. I love riding sports bikes and the feeling of satisfaction when I can control it as I want. Bikes at the time were very fast but they never turned like a race bike. The brief was to create a sports bike with total control that was easy to ride. This was my world; my ideal bike."

To achieve that, a compact size and ultralight weight were deemed key, with Baba setting a target of 190kg (the Yamaha was 209kg, the GSX-R a whopping 226kg) and demanding parts be redesigned rather than be too heavy. It also resulted in the first prototype, in late 1989: a 750.

"We designed the chassis first and the bike was a CBR750RR," remembered Baba. "But it was decided this would be way too

BELOW: The size of a 600 with the performance of a 1000, that was the revolutionary mantra of the first FireBlade, the CBR900RR, in 1992. HONDA

Price new	£7,390
Engine	893cc liquid cooled DOHC transverse four
Power	122bhp @ 10,500rpm
Torque	65lb-ft @ 85,00rpm
Frame	Aluminium twin spar
Suspension	45mm telescopic forks (F), monoshock (R)
Brakes	2 x 296mm discs (F), 220mm disc (R)
Tyres	130/70 x 16 (F), 180/55 x 18 (R)
Dry weight	185kg
Top speed	165mph

similar to our own RC30 and VFR750F, so we looked at 1000cc but that was too like our CBR1000F. We then realised that if we kept the bore but stroked the motor, we would get 893cc."

That was just the start. With the bike already internally referred to as 'Lightning', Baba's team underwent a further three years of uncompromising development with lightness the focus – sometimes in surprising areas.

"The CBR750RR had a 17-inch front wheel," Baba recalled. "But with the 900 we saw we could have same height with a 16-inch wheel and tyre and have better handling, quick turning but lighter weight."

The front suspension was equally unconventional. Inverted forks were becoming fashionable in the early 1990s, with Suzuki's 1990 GSX-R750L a superbike pioneer. But Baba, never one for trends, knew they were also heavier than traditional forks and refused to put them on the bike. There were even holes in the fairing which further reduced weight.

While, towards the end of its development, with concerns raised about creating a new, confusing 900cc class, it was decided to give prominence to its Lightning name, clumsily translated first into French, then English as FireBlade...

The result, the 1992 CBR900RR FireBlade, at just 1.8kg heavier than Honda's CBR600F2 but with litre-class capacity, was effectively the size of a 600 with the performance of a 1000.

It was even more radical to ride – manageable, unintimidating, even docile at low speed, the 'Blade was

ABOVE: Being a 900, Honda's new baby was initially ineligible for racing in the then 750cc superbike formula, although by the late 1990s it raced at the TT. HONDA

BELOW: The FireBlade was the brainchild of first-time motorcycle project leader, Tadao Baba who went on to lead all subsequent 'Blades up to 2004. HONDA

simply ballistic, explosive, dynamic and yet nimble with its throttle wide open – so much so that with its quick-steering 16in front wheel, some feared it was too flighty.

And yet it all worked – and then some. At the world press launch at Phillip Island, Australia, in early 1992 it caused a sensation. Its 122bhp and 185kg delivering 'superbike performance in a 600cc package' that ran rings round its heavyweight rivals and dominated the sales charts.

Soon after, in its first UK test, *Bike* magazine wrote: "If you want the quickest A-B road bike around, this is it. No contest. What it also is for me, however, is the most exhilarating, sexiest sports bike around by a country mile; a much more forgiving, more practical day to day bike than you could possibly imagine and, possibly, THE bike I want more than any other."

Instead, the 'Blade's only failing was on track where, TT apart, it never had any significant success. As a 900 it neither qualified for the 750cc superbike formula nor had the power to match lightened 1000cc-plus racers.

Nor was it a flash in the pan. While Honda's rivals set about playing catch-up (the first to achieve that was Yamaha's R1 in 1998, six years later with its project leader admitting the 'Blade was an inspiration), Baba successively updated his 'Blade.

The 'Foxeye' came in 1994. As there obviously wasn't much wrong with the original, Honda wisely resisted wholesale changes with its successor. Dubbed the 'Foxeye', due to its redesigned headlights, it was refined with updated bodywork, the addition of a compression damping adjuster to the front forks and a host of all minor modifications. Also available in an iconic

The fourth generation saw the biggest changes yet

'Urban Tiger' colour scheme (which was later revived on the 2012 machine), this remains one of the most revered and collectable of all 'Blades, second only to the original.

For its third incarnation in 1996, the CBR900RR-T/V FireBlade was more powerful and lighter, too, but for some it lost a little of its 'edge'. A 1mm larger bore took capacity to 918cc helping raise output to 128bhp. At the same time, a new, lighter stainless exhaust combined with a reshaped tank (which eliminated the need for a fuel pump) help cut weight to 183kg. Finally, along with the slightly reshaped tank, there was a new seat unit, the most obvious visual giveaway being the shift to two air vents from one each side. This, along with the tank, meant the riding position was altered slightly, being more upright, roomy and, well, soft almost…

In 1998, the fourth generation CBR900RR-W/X FireBlade saw the biggest changes yet but was still completely overshadowed by the simultaneous launch of Yamaha's all-new R1. Just like the original 'Blade in 1992, the 150bhp R1 set new standards for power, lightness and agility, finally usurping Honda's game changer. The 'Blade itself, meanwhile, despite 2bhp more power and even less weight was, next to the R1, almost a sports tourer, being roomy, comfortable and practical. It was time for the 'Blade to go back to basics…

Honda's response, the 2000-1 CBR900RR Y/1 FireBlade (or 929 as it became known), had 151bhp thanks to an enlarged, 929cc (and now fuel-injected) motor, complete with an all-new frame that had the swingarm mounted to the back of the gearbox, inverted forks and, at

last, a 17in front wheel. But, despite being a great bike and a definite return to form for the FireBlade, it wasn't quite enough to usurp the all-conquering Yamaha.

With the 929 coming so close to the R1, Baba's team must have been confident its next update – the sixth – would finally reclaim top spot. Unfortunately for Honda, Suzuki by then had launched the first GSX-R1000, which shook up the class. That shouldn't take away from the fact that the 2002 CBR900RR-2/3 FireBlade, or '954' as it is now known, is considered one of the best 'Blades of all. An extra 1mm on the bore took capacity to 954cc and power was up again. Road handling, though sharp, was considered the best in the class, the styling was handsome, and there was

typical Honda class and refinement everywhere. The 954 may not have been outright top dog, but it was – and still is – the thinking man's superbike. It was also the last 'Blade to have its design overseen by Tadao Baba before his retirement.

The 2004-5 Honda CBR1000RR 4/5 Fireblade was the first 'Blade after the retirement of Tadao Baba (hence the capital 'B' in its name being replaced by a smaller 'b', as a mark of respect) and was also the first full 1000, partly as WSB was changing its rules to suit full litre-capacity machines. It was unashamedly inspired by Honda's new RC211V MotoGP machine. The result, with 169bhp, sharper handling still due to its new die-cast frame, was the most potent and racy 'Blade yet, although not quite as explosive as the then Yamaha R1 and new Kawasaki ZX-10R.

At first glance it looked like the previous machine, the eighth generation 'Blade, the 2006 CBR1000RR-6/7 Fireblade, was significantly different and much more refined. Engine modifications included new porting and different valves to boost torque and raise power by 3bhp, larger discs added braking power, while the bodywork, though broadly similar

LEFT: Baba 'San' was also fundamentally involved with succeeding FireBlade models. Here he is with the fourth-generation version. HONDA

RIGHT: Virtually everything on the 'Blade was about saving weight – hence the holes in both the fairing cowling and belly pan. HONDA

BELOW: Baba 'San', right, now retired, with the leaders of more recent Fireblades on the occasion of its 25th anniversary at Honda's Collection Hall in Japan. HONDA

to before, was all new, sleeker and more refined. As a road bike it was brilliant, on track it became the only model of the 'Blade to win a world superbike title (with Brit James Toseland in 2007), and today this variant, due to its refined ride, classy build and classic, handsome good looks, is considered one of the best of the breed.

Honda's superbike received a complete makeover once again to produce the radical-looking 2008 CBR1000RR 8/9 Fireblade. Gone were the under-seat pipe and angular styling, replaced with side-mounted exhausts and more bluff lines that weren't universally liked. That said, now with 175bhp and a lighter chassis, it was a sublime handler on track and on road (and particularly at the TT) and remains a brilliantly balanced road sportster for connoisseurs to this day.

In 2009, although outwardly similar, the 'Blade was improved further with the addition of sophisticated Combined-ABS brakes, while in 2010 it received subtle modifications such as a lighter flywheel and more compact radiator fan motor. By now, however, although still a great road bike, the 'Blade had fallen far behind new class leaders, such as BMW's S1000RR.

The 2012 CBR1000RR-12 was effectively an update of the 2008 machine rather than an all-new bike. Launched to mark the 'Blade's 20th anniversary, it received a host of improvements, not least a face-lifted nose. Other modifications included a revised front and rear suspension including new 'Big Piston' forks, more lightweight 12-spoke wheels and a new LCD dash. None of it, however,

not even the introduction of an Öhlins-equipped 'SP' version in 2014, was enough to keep up with the latest ZX-10R, S1000RR and, in 2015, Yamaha's all-new YZF-R1.

Honda's first all-new Fireblade since 2008 was launched in 2017. Available in three guises —stock, Öhlins, Brembos and more SP, and WSB homologation special SP2 — it produced a competitive 189bhp-plus, had as sporty a chassis as any, and, for the first time, came with electronic rider aids such as traction control, power modes and cornering ABS, and yet it was now too extreme, for some, without being the track winner Honda craved, something that was still not sorted (but was improved) with a 2019 revision.

Which is why, for 2020, the 'Blade was reinvented

again, becoming even more revvy, powerful and sophisticated and, via an SP version, finally becoming at least close to competitive on track.

Although today's Fireblade may not be the dominant force or game changer it once was, it remains pretty much the definitive Japanese superbike. But that 1992 original was literally something else. ■

BELOW: Honda's original 1992 CBR900RR FireBlade is now considered so revolutionary and significant, good ones are prized as genuine modern classics. HONDA

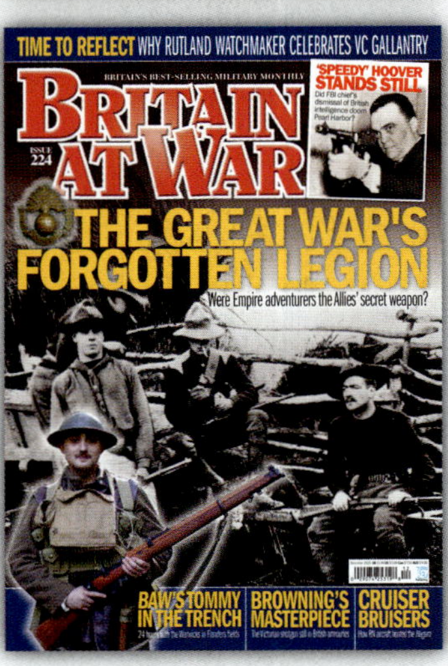

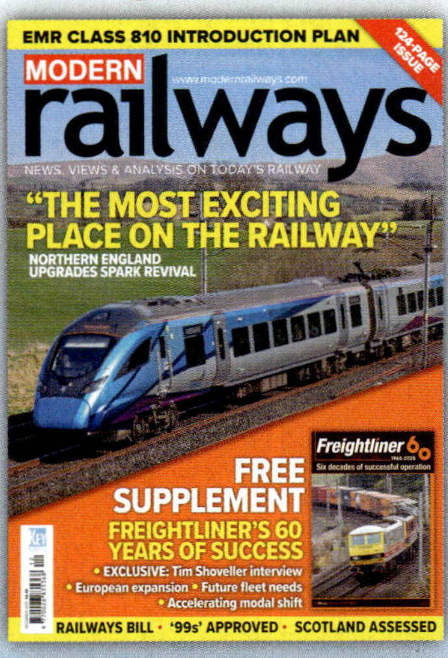

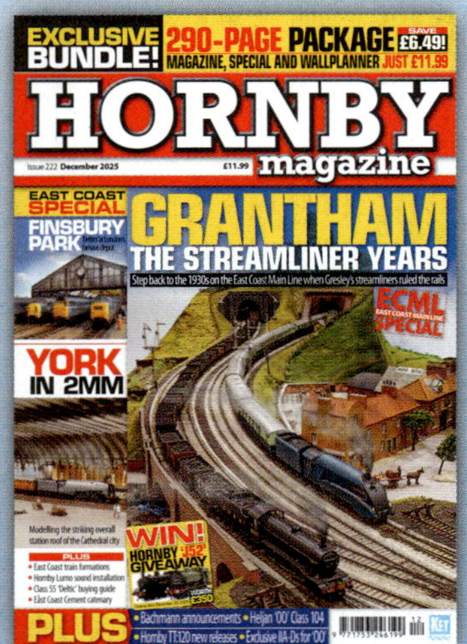

Enjoy one of our many titles today!

SUBSCRIBE TODAY!

Our historic and informative magazines cover a wide array of topics from around the world. From Aviation and Aircraft to Modelling, Public Transport and Railways to Classic Vehicles, Military History and more, we're sure you'll find something you can't put down.

With Digital and Print magazine subscriptions allowing you to find out more about your favourite topic in the format that is most comfortable for you, why not treat yourself to a subscription that'll take your interest to the next level today?

SOME REASONS TO SUBSCRIBE TO ONE OF OUR FANTASTIC MAGAZINES

» **EXCLUSIVE** Subscriber offers on the *Key Publishing* Shop » **SAVE** over buying individual issues

» **DELIVERED DIRECT** to your door » **BE THE FIRST** to read the latest features

» **SUBSCRIBER DISCOUNTS** on *Key Publishing* event tickets

Scan the QR code TODAY to order direct from our shop!

shop.keypublishing.com/collections/all-subscriptions

or call **+44 (0)1780 480404** (Lines open 9.00-5.30, Monday-Friday GMT)

1992 HONDA
NR750

The oval-pistoned production superbike that celebrated the wildest GP racer of all

SPECIFICATIONS	
Price new	£38,500
Engine	747.7cc liquid cooled DOHC oval piston V4
Power	125bhp @ 14,000rpm
Torque	50.5lb-ft @ 11,000rpm
Frame	Aluminium twin spar
Suspension	45mm telescopic forks (F), monoshock (R)
Brakes	2 x 310mm discs (F), 220mm disc (R)
Tyres	130/70 x 16 (F), 180/55 x 18 (R)
Dry weight	220kg
Top speed	160mph

For Honda, 1992 may be most associated with the debut of the first FireBlade, but it also saw the unveiling of an arguably even more significant machine, the NR750.

Although only 300 were built, it had a price five times that of the 'Blade's £7,390 and its performance was hardly any better, the NR was a technological wonder that showcased Honda's engineering, celebrated its oval piston project, and featured inspirational design elements including under seat exhausts and digital instrumentation years before Ducati's 916 and Yamaha's R1. In short, without the NR750, 1990s motorcycling would not have been the same.

The NR750 was the final fanfare for Honda's NR – New Racer –

ABOVE: Although never conceived as a track eligible superbike, the NR750 was the culmination of Honda's revolutionary oval piston NR racer programme. HONDA

project, which started with the NR500. In 1979, 12 years after quitting GPs due to FIM cost-cutting rules which restricted 500s to four cylinders and 250/350s to twins (so banning innovative engineering such as Honda's 1966 RC166 250cc six), Honda returned to 500 GPs but, with four-cylinder two strokes, such as Suzuki's RG500, dominant, Honda decided to compete with its preferred four-stroke. To compensate for the 'strokers' inherent extra power stroke advantage, Honda effectively created a 'faux' V8 – a V4 but with 'oval' cylinders each with two conrods, eight valves per cylinder, twin plugs and, in theory, twice the power.

It was an immensely ambitious project and one which, despite a vast budget and development

team, never quite succeeded. The debut of the first 100bhp NR500 0X racer in 1979's British GP ended in ignominy when both bikes barely qualified, Mick Grant crashed on his own oil at the first corner, and the second entrant, ridden by Takazumi Katayama, blew its engine after seven laps.

Honda persevered but the 'Never Ready' 500 was also never

RIGHT: The 1979 NR500 GP racer had been conceived to be a four stroke that could compete on equal terms with the then dominant two strokes. HONDA

BOTTOM: Other pioneering tech on the 750 included under seat exhausts and the world's first (part) digital LCD motorcycle dash. HONDA

BELOW: As such, its V4 engine employed oval pistons and eight valves, plus two conrods per piston to mimic the dimensions of a V8. HONDA

a success. In 1980 the 1X achieved 120bhp, with 1982's 2X 125, by then, however, after three years of expensive failure, Honda had decided to race its new NS500 two-stroke triple. And that bike's immediate success forced the NR into the background.

But it wasn't the end of the NR story. Those later bhp figures showed potential, Honda remained desperate to prove its oval-piston concept a winner and HRC came up with the idea of an NR750 endurance racer – a 750cc oval-piston V4 in an RVF chassis which, although only entered in two races in 1987, shone brighter than ever before.

Then came the NR's final 'hurrah' – the 1992 NR750 (RC40) road bike, developed by a team led by Mitsuyoshi Kohama, (who later designed Honda's RC211V MotoGP racer) and intended to showcase Honda technology like no production road bike had before.

First teased in August 1990 as travelling marshal bikes at the Suzuka 8 Hour, it was a further two years before the NR750 was launched for general sale.

Its engine was based on the NR750 racer, while its chassis comprised a titanium-coated aluminium twin-spar frame, single-sided swinger and Honda's first 'upside-down' forks. The exhaust exited under the seat, twin radiators were side mounted, there was carbon fibre bodywork, an iridium-coated screen, combined analogue/digital LED instrumentation (six years before the R1), indicators integrated into mirrors, magnesium wheels, and even bespoke brakes and key.

In short, the NR750 looked like nothing else and had technology years in advance of anything else. In building it, Honda claimed over 200 patents, 50 for the oval piston rings alone.

In truth, of course, it was also something of a folly. Heavy and with only 125bhp, its performance was no better than the 'Blade; at £38,000 it was never likely to sell and just 322 were made – 220 in 1992 (20 being the 100bhp RC41 variant for the French and Japanese markets), plus 102 more in 1993 before production was terminated.

Did Honda care? Probably not. The NR750 had served its purpose in proving its oval piston concept could work and in cementing Honda's reputation as the leading two-wheeled engineering company on the planet.

"When I look back at it, I'm not sure if we were experimenting with cutting-edge technologies or obsessed with foolish ideas," recalled Toshimitsu Yoshimura, an engineer involved in the NR500.

"[But] to create anything, you must put your heart and soul to it," he added. "The development of oval piston engines impressed that upon me, as well as on the other young engineers."

The NR impressed others, too, not least Italian design legend

> **66 The NR750 had technology years in advance of anything else 99**

Massimo Tamburini. "When I saw the NR750 I thought it was going to be the future of motorcycling," he admitted years later. "I didn't want to copy it with the 916 but I wanted the 916 to look like it with sharper lines. At that point we had been experimenting with other exhaust positions, to the side of the bike like the 888 and at different heights, but when I saw the NR, I tried under the seat and it felt right."

The NR750 may not have been a commercial success, but design appreciation doesn't get any greater than that.

And while the 500 version may not have succeeded in GPs and the NR750 endurance racer also missed out, the NR did eventually make it into the record books when Honda decided to use it to attempt some publicity generating world speed records. At Italy's Nardo speed bowl in 1993, a lightened, tuned NR750, making 150bhp at 15,500rpm and weighing just 180kg (compared to the standard bike's hefty 222kg) was ridden by then Honda GP rider Loris Capirossi where it hit 200mph to set new flying mile, flying kilometre and standing start mile, and 10km world records during a specially organised Honda PR event.

Finally, the NR had been proved to be a winner after all. Today, meanwhile, the NR750 is one of the rarest, most collectable Japanese machines of all. ■

1994 DUCATI 916

Tamburini's masterpiece which dominated world superbikes for nearly a decade

Motoring buffs often claim that a true classic must be innovative, beautiful, exotic, expensive, exclusive and have achieved genuine racing success. In the world of superbikes of the late 20th century, no motorcycle was more qualified in all of that than the Ducati 916.

Its single-sided swing arm and under seat exhausts started a new design trend (even though its acclaimed designer Massimo Tamburini later admitted both were inspired by Honda's NR750). Its striking, chisel-nosed purity won design plaudits across the globe; as Ducati's flagship superbike it was exotic, expensive and exclusive and, by the end of the '90s, it hadn't just won in the world superbike championship – it had dominated it, winning first time out with British hero Carl Fogarty before reclaiming the crown four more times up to 2000, with three going to 'Foggy' alone.

And yet, even though the 916 was the successor to Ducati's 888/851, which itself had claimed a WSB hat-trick up to 1993, no one had really predicted the scale of the 916's success.

A result of a collaboration of three of motorcycling's greatest brains, Tamburini, Cagiva owner Claudio Castiglioni and chief engineer Massimo Bordi, the 916 helped drag Ducati out of the antiquated state it found itself in as the 1990s began

SPECIFICATIONS

Price new	£11,800
Engine	916cc liquid cooled Desmodromic 90° V-twin
Power	114bhp @ 9,000rpm
Torque	65lb-ft @ 7,000rpm
Frame	Tubular steel trellis
Suspension	43mm telescopic forks (F), monoshock (R)
Brakes	2 x 320mm discs (F), 220mm disc (R)
Tyres	120/70 x 17 (F), 190/50 x 17 (R)
Dry weight	198kg
Top speed	160mph

BELOW: The man and his machine. The 916 was styled by design genius Massimo Tamburini, formerly of Bimota and later behind the MV Agusta 750 F4.

DUCATI

and into a new era of sustained success and worldwide fame.

Recognising Ducati was a brand built on race victories, owner Castiglioni approached Cagiva Design Director Tamburini (who had previously formed Bimota, the 'ta' in its name is for Tamburini), with a simple request for the 851/888's successor.

"Castiglioni asked for another breakthrough bike," recalled Tamburini in one of the last interviews before his death in 2014. "He said, 'I don't want an old Ducati, and I don't want a Japanese bike'..."

The result, with Bordi's engineering, Tamburini's styling (via his Cagiva Research Centre in San Marino) and developed in complete secrecy, was a revelation, with sufficient performance to win six of the next eight WSB crowns (including those by the 996 and 998 derivatives), a slim, angular, aggressive style which won design awards across the globe defined by a Honda NR750-inspired rear end with single-sided swing arm and

twin under seat exhausts, and with the whole thing generating sufficient sales to ensure Ducati's survival.

Tamburini also later explained the Honda influence: "When I saw the NR750 [as a concept bike at the 1989 Tokyo Motor Show] I thought it was going to be the future of motorcycling," the great man remembered. "I didn't want to copy it, but I wanted the 916 to look like it with sharper lines... to look aggressive but also classical – and the two exhausts under the seat looked perfect."

Incidentally, those under seat exhaust pipes were actually a relatively late change to the 916's design. Initially it was intended to use side-mounted pipes and so in this respect the 916's baby sister,

The angular, more compact, sharper 916 made the outgoing 888 immediately look bloated and overweight. DUCATI

the second-generation Cagiva Mito 125 that also appeared in 1994 and shares near-identical styling, is arguably closer to the original design.

The inspiration for the 916's sharper lines and slit-like headlights, however, came from elsewhere. The advent of projector-beam headlights – which first appeared in cars in the latter half of the 1980s – gave bike designers the freedom to move away from the traditional round or rectangular lights that previously defined front-end styling and to experiment with new shapes. The idea of two slit-shaped lights may have become a common one on modern machines, but in 1994 the 916 was a pioneer.

Those lights were needed because Tamburini's styling also borrowed heavily from the work done by Pierre Terblanche on the Ducati Supermono single-cylinder racer, which first introduced the arrow-shaped side profile to the nose that the 916 would later take on.

The engine, meanwhile, was Bordi's 'Desmoquattro' liquid-cooled, four-valve, 90° 'L-twin' from the successful 888 but taken up to 916cc by a 2mm longer stroke resulting in its power also going up from 100 to 114bhp. The chassis, meanwhile, with a new tubular steel trellis frame by Tamburini, and despite its new, heavier, single-sided swing arm, was overall lighter than the 851 (by 4kg), shorter (by 20mm) and sharper.

And in October 1993, the 916 made its debut at the Milan Motorcycle Show, immediately becoming an icon of Ducati style, ►

an instant contender for the biggest superbike prize of all, the World Superbike Championship, and much more besides.

In truth, on the road some of that extreme spec was a pain. The 916 was so sporty, stiff and uncompromising, it was also cramped and uncomfortable. At first however, that didn't matter. On track, where the 916 was launched (at Misano, Italy, in February 1994), the press were blown away. Britain's *Bike* magazine boldly claiming "Carl Fogarty WILL win the World Superbike Championship this year" even though the 916 itself wasn't deemed sufficiently significant to be pictured on its cover (told you no one saw the 916 coming).

American *Cycle World* magazine, meanwhile, in July of that year, wrote: "The 916 is an open invitation to enjoy state-of-the-art motorcycle thinking, engineering, design and performance. In the US it will carry list prices of $14,500, a thousand bucks more than last year's 888. You don't have to be a genius to figure out that anyone who cares about exotic motorcycles will find this a screaming deal."

It was also on the track where the 916 would rack up its greatest honours. With its 'grunty', explosive and droningly evocative engine blending with ultra nimble handling, it proved pretty much unbeatable in superbike race series across the globe: as well as 'Foggy's 1994 WSB title, it won the 1994 American AMA superbike crown, 1995 British superbike series, and others besides. In magazine polls the 916 swept the board, too.

> ## 66 *It proved pretty much unbeatable in superbike race series across the globe* 99

And, of course, all of that was just the start. Financial difficulties and production delays meant that, although 916 demand was high, production was slow and low, and the first customer 916s didn't reach buyers until mid-1994, in 'monoposto' (single seat) Strada form making 114hp. A higher-spec 916 SP was also introduced later that year with a claimed 126hp thanks to a significantly different, twin-injector version of the Desmoquattro engine with race-oriented internals.

That 1994 Strada was replaced the following year by the twin-seat Biposto and also saw the debut of the first 916 Senna – a project that had been instigated before Ayrton Senna's death in 1994. That bike combined the standard Strada/Biposto spec engine with a handful of uprated chassis parts from the SP, along with a black paint scheme, red wheels and a smattering of carbon fibre body panels. Just 300 were made, but later 'Senna II' and 'Senna III' models would boost that total.

In 1996 the focus was on racing, and while the basic 916 Biposto street bike wasn't updated, Ducati spent much of the early years of 916 production constantly fiddling with high-spec, limited edition versions in order to homologate racing parts. Duly, in 1996 Ducati introduced the 916 SPS, featuring a larger 996cc engine and built even smaller numbers of a very rare model called the 955SP with a 955cc capacity. (Ducati had been racing with a 955cc engine in the World Superbike Championship since 1994 but needed to build 50 roadgoing examples with the same 96mm bore to be allowed to use the 955cc motor in AMA Superbike racing in America.)

Racing-inspired changes continued in 1997 with the introduction of the 916 SPS. While this nominally added just one letter to the name of its predecessor, in reality it was a very different beast with a largely new engine with redesigned crankcases to allow the motor to be bored out to 996cc, so pushing it nearer to the 1000cc limit then prevailing in superbike racing. Power for the new 996cc motor rose to 134hp and a second run of 916 Sennas also appeared that year.

The big news for 1998, at least in the UK, was the introduction of the Ducati 916 'Foggy Replica'. Ostensibly a replica tribute to Carl Fogarty – which is why it was aimed at the British market – the Foggy Rep was also a sneaky move to homologate a revised frame and airbox for WSB racing. With 202 made, Ducati produced just enough to satisfy WSB production minimums at the time.

As the end of the millennium neared, the Biposto version of the 916, which had missed out on most of the race-inspired updates of the previous few years, was

ABOVE: It was in the hands of another Brit, Carl Fogarty, that the 916 shone brightest, carrying him to four WSB crowns and six in total. DUCATI

LEFT: Other racers who had the 916 to thank for their world superbike championship titles included Australians Troy Corser and, here, Troy Bayliss. DUCATI

As for the decade-long success of the 916/996/998, quite simply, no other superbike came close – then or now.

The fact most motorcycling mortals couldn't afford one didn't really matter. Nor does the perhaps surprise revelation that the 916 wasn't built in the numbers many expect. Just 2,000 'Monopostos' were made in 1994 along with 700 Bipostos, 199 Ss and 310 SPs. In 1995 there were around 500 Monopostos, 2000 Bipostos and 300 Sennas, and over the course of the 916's life up to 1998, just 38 Factory racers were made.

What does matter was that the 916 was a strikingly beautiful 'poster bike' for a generation, with the performance and pose to match its prestige.

In racing, although undoubtedly the biggest beneficiary of regulations which favoured 1000cc V-twins, the 916 still over-delivered, winning the world superbike crown for Fogarty in its first year, repeating the feat the following year, winning again in 1996 (this time with Troy Corser after Foggy moved to Honda) then again with the Brit in 1998 and 1999 (by then on the renamed 996).

Today, as a result of all of that, the 916 (and its derivatives) is not only revered as one of the best bikes of the 1990s but as one of the best superbikes of all time and the bike which also restored Ducati as king of the European superbike builders, a status the Italian brand has retained to this day. ■

finally readdressed in 1999, being transformed in the process into the new 996. The new number reflected its enlarged engine capacity which now matched that of the previous 916 SPS (and became the 996 SPS in 1999).

While by 2000, although the 916 didn't officially exist in Ducati's range anymore, the subsequent models still tend to generically go under the '916' banner as they were effectively modified versions of the original. That year saw yet another capacity change as the 996 SPS was replaced by the 996R, which, despite its name, actually displaced a capacity of 998cc and was the first of Ducati's Testastretta ('narrow head') V-twins. This design, with a narrower angle between the valves, allowed a bigger bore and shorter stroke, providing racing versions with a substantial power increase.

While, finally, with the introduction of the 998 in 2002, the bike's name caught up with its capacity again as the 998cc Testastretta engine spread across the entire Ducati superbike range. This final fling for the iconic, Tamburini-designed machine also received refreshed styling, with new, flat fairing sides replacing the vented originals so making for the smoothest '916' yet.

Also with the 998, Ducati adopted the naming convention it has retained to this day. Namely, a 'basic' 998 was joined by a higher-spec, Öhlins-suspended 998 S, with the trio topped by a homologation-special, 'race' version, the 'R'. Of course, as is also still repeated to this day, this still left room for limited edition, 'special' versions, which included Ben Bostrom and Troy Bayliss replicas. There was also a green '998 Matrix' to commemorate the bike's appearance in *The Matrix Reloaded* movie. While, finally, and ten years after the original 916's launch, the 2004 998 Final Edition was sold alongside its replacement, the Pierre Terblanche-designed Ducati 999, which had been revealed in 2003. That bike, however, is another story.

BELOW: At its world press launch at Misano in February 1994 the 916 caused a sensation. Pictured is the author, who tested it for *Bike* magazine. DUCATI

1994 HONDA
RVF750R RC45

Honda's eagerly anticipated successor to the RC30, which didn't quite deliver…

The WSB-targeted, homologation special RVF750R (or RC45 as it quickly became known) was launched in 1994 as the long-awaited and highly anticipated successor to Honda's first all-conquering V4 superbike, the RC30. And although closely related to the RC30 in being a 90° V4 with gear-driven cams in an aluminium twin spar frame which featured a single-sided swing arm, it was actually all-new and co-developed by Honda's racing division, HRC, and Honda R&D.

Just a short time earlier, the extremely complex NR750 had been released for road use and some of the technology of the NR750 was carried across to the RC45. This included its fuel injection system, clutch, sprag clutch and even the 16in front wheel size.

The engine was significantly different to the RC30's, too. The RC45 had shorter stroke, more oversquare dimensions of 72mm bore and 46mm stroke compared to the RC30's 70 x 48.6mm, and this allowed the RC45 higher rpm while maintaining equal piston speed. Where the RC30 had used roller bearings on the camshafts, the RC45 used more conventional plain bearings. And while the RC30 used a piston with one compression ring plus an oil control ring to reduce friction (which was effective for racing but resulted in increased oil consumption on the road), the RC45 changed to the more conventional two compression ring system, also with an oil control ring.

Other engine architecture changes included a move from a centre gear-drive mechanism to crank-camshaft drive; the valve angle was tightened from 38° on

ABOVE: Despite the hefty price tag and the dominance of Ducati's 916, racing versions of the RC453 did prove successful, if not in WSB, then at the TT and in world endurance. HONDA

The RC45 was intended as Honda's improved replacement for the hugely successful RC30 with a new engine, chassis, fuel injection and more. HONDA

SPECIFICATIONS

Price new	£17,780
Engine	749cc liquid cooled DOHC 90° V4
Power	118bhp @ 12,000rpm
Torque	56lb-ft @ 10,000rpm
Frame	Aluminium twin spar
Suspension	41mm telescopic forks (F), monoshock (R)
Brakes	2 x 310mm discs (F), 220mm disc (R)
Tyres	130/60 x 16 (F), 190/50 x 17 (R)
Dry weight	189kg
Top speed	161mph

the RC30 to 26 with the RC45; intake ports were shorter and intake valves 2mm larger. But probably the most significant change of all was with the adoption of Programmed Fuel Injection (PFI), a system very similar to that on the NR750, instead of the RC30's carburettors, which potentially allowed extremely high power at high rpm.

Conversely, the RC45's gearbox was very similar to that of the RC30 and even had the same gear ratios with only primary and secondary ratios changed. The one-way sprag clutch was also carried over from the RC30 but was of NR750 design and was a forerunner to today's slipper clutches, affording a slight amount of slip on overrun in an attempt to stop the back wheel from locking. The clutch plates were also from the NR750 and were much larger in diameter compared to those of the RC30.

Another 'carry over' from the NR was the RC45's brakes. The newcomer's front discs were the same 310mm items from the oval-pistoned wonder with four piston calipers. While the frame and overall chassis dimensions of the RC45 were little changed from the RC30, too. The steering angle was sharpened by 0.5 degree, the wheelbase increased by a few millimetres, the swing arm lengthened slightly, and front height was dropped by 4mm. Instead, the major change was the motor's position in the frame, being moved significantly forward.

Cynics will say the RC45 wasn't the success it should have been. In stock trim its V4 motor produced just 118bhp when Yamaha's YZF already had seven more. With a price tag of $27,500 in the US (£18,000 in the

UK), it was prohibitively expensive (*Performance Bikes* magazine in its cover test of June 1994, went so far as to brand it a 'Waste of money') and it never matched the racing roll of honour of its predecessor, the RC30, infamously failing to provide reigning world superbike champion Carl Fogarty with any more crowns, despite two attempts and ultimately claiming its sole WSB title in 1997 via John Kocinski.

But neither was that the whole story. That 118bhp was something of a red herring. In full race-prepped kitted form (the RC45 was a homologation special racer, after all), its output was nearer 150 and, although heavy compared to the rival twins, its spec, including titanium rods and fuel injection, blew most rivals away.

The RC45 also had more race success than most onlookers gave it credit for. As well as Kocinski's WSB crown, Miguel Duhamel won the 1995 US AMA Superbike title and the 1996 Daytona 200 on an RC45, while Ben Bostrom won the 1998 AMA crown. The RC45 also proved a huge success in endurance racing, winning the FIM world crown six times, and was massively successful at the Isle of Man TT.

As a road bike, although sublimely refined and mouth-wateringly exotic and exquisite, the RC45 was also something of a white elephant. Its high first gear was intrusive, its road legal 118bhp was nothing special, it was considered big and bulky next to the new breed of V-twins and, at £18,000, it was twice the price of a Fireblade, 50% more than a Ducati 916 and as a result, largely irrelevant.

Overall, however, the biggest failure – if that's what it was – of

ABOVE: Today, like its RC30 predecessor, the RC45 remains one of the most exclusive, impressive and collectable Japanese superbikes of all. HONDA

BELOW: Although incredibly sophisticated, it proved underpowered (without a race kit), heavy and, as a road bike, was prohibitively expensive. HONDA

the RC45, was that it didn't quite live up to its own hype. As the successor to the RC30 but in an environment that now favoured the lighter, larger capacity, more powerful V-twins, the RC45 was on a hiding to nothing from the outset. It was never going to dominate on road or track as its predecessor had done so spectacularly and Honda themselves ultimately had to admit defeat and produce its own 1000cc V-twin (the 2000 VTR1000SP-1), to get the WSB success it craved.

None of that reflects too harshly on the RC45. It may never have quite been the race success Honda hoped for, but it remains one of the most exquisite, advanced V4 superbikes ever built, is now viewed as a beautiful, exotic swan song for Honda's V4 homologation specials, representing a peak era for superbike development, and, with very limited numbers built, remains one of the most highly prized homologation special superbikes of all. ∎

1996 SUZUKI
GSX-R750 SRAD

The all-new, beam frame 'Gixxer' that set the new Suzuki standard

The SRAD (Suzuki Ram Air Direct) not only saw the Suzuki GSX-R750 return to form after losing its way in the early to mid-1990s, but it was also effectively the last great 750cc superbike. Along with the change in the superbike racing regulations from 750 to 1000cc, it helped cause the extinction of all rivals before, after a series of updates, surviving as the definitive 750 superbike up to the 2010s. (After the RC45 and YZF/R7, neither Honda nor Yamaha produced a superbike 750, while Kawasaki's ZXR/ZX-7R only lived on to 2003.)

A bold, clean sheet design which finally replaced the 'Gixxer's traditional cradle frame for a then dominant twin spar design, the SRAD was Suzuki's first truly modern GSX-R since the 1985 original and represented Suzuki's unfettered bid to return to the top of the superbike tree. And, with inspiration from the 500 grand prix, a screaming, all-new, ram air-assisted transverse four, ultra-nimble steering and an aerodynamic

ABOVE: After years of WSB uncompetitiveness with its later GSX-R750s, Suzuki returned to the top table of production racing with its all-new GSX-R750WT.
SUZUKI

SPECIFICATIONS

Price new	£8,999
Engine	749cc liquid cooled DOHC transverse four
Power	128bhp @ 12,000rpm
Torque	59.3lb-ft @ 10,000rpm
Frame	Aluminium twin spar
Suspension	43mm inverted telescopic forks (F), monoshock (R)
Brakes	2 x 317mm discs (F), 220mm disc (R)
Tyres	120/70 x 17 (F), 190/50 x 17 (R)
Dry weight	179kg
Top speed	167.4mph

ABOVE: Although arguably the best of the Japanese 750cc four-cylinder superbikes, it was still not quite a match for the 1000cc V-twin Ducati 916. SUZUKI

LEFT: Also known as the SRAD, the new GSX-R took inspiration from Kevin Schwantz's 1993 grand prix world championship winning RGV500. SUZUKI

RIGHT: The result was compact, slim, light, aerodynamic (due to its distinctive seat hump) and, with an all-new 128bhp engine, fast. SUZUKI

profile more slippery than any rival, it very nearly succeeded.

Suzuki's GSX-R750 already had an impressive history up to 1996. The 1985 original, which had been inspired by Suzuki's then world championship F1 works machine, effectively created the modern racer replica while its successors mostly improved on that bike's template of aluminium box section cradle frame with a revvy, oil then water-cooled transverse four.

But with the 750, after 1990, no longer truly competitive in superbike racing and with a new generation of ultralight 1000s headlined by 1992's Honda CBR900RR FireBlade demoting the GSX-R's 1100cc big brother to dinosaur status, by the mid 1990s it was clear that the traditional GSX-R's time was up.

The SRAD changed all that.

Inspired by Kevin Schwantz's 1993 world championship-winning RGV500 (many of whose dimensions it mirrored), the SRAD was altogether more aggressive, powerful, lighter and compact. Its biggest performance gains over its predecessor were that its weight was down by 20kg to 179kg, the same as the 1985 original and which put it in the same weight bracket as most 600s of the time, and its class-leading 128bhp, which was closer to the 1000s of the era than rival 750s and which actually bested Honda's then CBR900RR, both in terms of peak horsepower and top speed.

The main ingredients in that transformation were the SRAD's all-new engine and its chassis.

The engine's liquid-cooled, transverse four-cylinder, double overhead cam, 16-valve layout may have been relatively conventional — but was more extreme in every respect. With a much more

'oversquare' 72mm bore x 46mm stroke configuration (the outgoing GSX-R750 had a 70 x 48.7mm setup), the SRAD sported a ridiculously high-revving 13,500rpm redline. It was also fed by a bank of Mikuni downdraft carbs (for the first two years of its design before being replaced by fuel injection) which featured electronically controlled slides for a smoother throttle response.

But the engine's biggest advance was SRAD. By featuring two large through-the-frame air ducts leading to the oversized airbox, the new Suzuki boasted the first true 'ram-air' system on a 750 superbike, helping boost peak power at high speed.

Along with its big, class-leading power, the new SRAD's motor was also pioneeringly small and compact. By positioning the cam chain on the end of the crank and mounting the alternator behind the crankshaft instead of on the end, the engine lost a full 30mm of width. The crankshaft also lost one set of main bearings — going from six to five — as part of the space-saving efforts. While another benefit of the narrow design was that the cylinder bores could be 5mm closer together, made possible by the use of nickel silicon carbide-plated aluminum cylinders, where the old model used iron press-in liners. Overall, the engine redesign alone shed a phenomenal 9kg.

The frame, too, although again on face value merely an 'AN Other'

> ## 66 Dimensions modelled on Schwantz's RGV 99

aluminium twin spar design, pushed the boundaries further than ever. Not satisfied with being Suzuki's first twin spar, the design not only saved more than 2kg over the old model, it doubled its overall torsional stiffness and enabled impressively compact dimensions modelled on those of Schwantz's RGV. Its wheelbase, for example, was the same just 1,400mm, with a rake of 24° degrees and 97mm of trail, which together made for seriously quick steering.

The new GSX-R's cycle parts and aerodynamics were class-leading, too. New Tokico six-piston brake calipers provided serious stopping power up front, a 6in-wide rim capable of carrying one of the first 190-section tyres debuted at the rear. The rear shock was a fully adjustable Showa piggyback unit and there was a similarly adjustable pair of ultra-beefy 43mm-diameter inverted forks at the nose. The ultra-slippery bodywork, meanwhile, complete with distinctive pillion 'hump', was wind-tunnel-developed and helped the SRAD slip its way to a 750 class-leading top speed.

And yet... it wasn't quite all enough for the SRAD to succeed as much as originally hoped. On the street, the new Suzuki may have quickly established itself as the sportiest 750, but in a class already dominated by Honda's 900cc FireBlade and shortly to be revolutionised further by Yamaha's upcoming 1000cc R1, it struggled to stand out.

On track, as a 750 four against the rampaging Ducati V-twins, the SRAD also struggled from the same miss-match in performance that had first plagued Honda's RC45 then later Yamaha's R7. In world superbike racing, for example, despite a factory-backed British team, it played second fiddle; while in the British equivalent it fared better but still never came out on top.

If the SRAD didn't 'quite' win on road or track, it certainly did in terms of re-establishing the GSX-R at the forefront of the superbike and sporting classes.

A 600 followed a year later; an improved 750 12 months after that and a new class-shattering 1000 in 2001, with all fundamentally relighting a 'GSX-R' fire that continues to this day. ∎

1997 TRIUMPH
T595 DAYTONA

The revived British brand gets in on the act with its first true superbike

The revival of historic British marque Triumph by industrialist John Bloor had been huge news and its first range of bikes, unveiled in 1991, had largely been a big success. However, those first machines, based on a modular system of interchangeable, heavyweight triples and fours in fairly crude but solid chassis, were never truly competitive with the best from Europe and Japan.

That all changed with the launch of Triumph's all-new T595 Daytona superbike in 1997.

In simple terms, the T595 was the machine with which reborn Triumph motorcycles came of age. Modern, good looking, fast and fine handling, the Daytona was the brand's first superbike which had been designed to compete head-on with the best from both Japan and Italy. And, although in truth ultimately not quite as good as either, the T595's style, performance, character and quality made it an initial big success, cemented the brand's status among motorcycling's elite and thus paved the way for a whole series of subsequent modern Triumphs that remain the backbone of the Hinckley-based company to this day.

Following Triumph's initial 'modular' range of triples and fours

SPECIFICATIONS	
Price new	£9,995
Engine	955cc liquid cooled DOHC transverse triple
Power	130bhp @ 10,200rpm
Torque	73.8lb-ft @ 8,300rpm
Frame	Aluminium tube trellis
Suspension	45mm telescopic forks (F), monoshock (R)
Brakes	2 x 320mm discs (F), 220mm disc (R)
Tyres	120/70 x 17 (F), 190/50 x 17 (R)
Dry weight	192.6kg
Top speed	158mph

from 1991, then its first Speed Triple 900 in 1994 (with which the revived brand famously 'found its mojo') and then its first push into the vital US market in 1995 with its all-new Thunderbird 900, it was time for Triumph's next big move.

The key factor in all of that was Bloor's decision to abandon the earlier modular concept in order to produce an all-new superbike capable of taking on, as Triumph

BELOW: The frame was in aluminium, the three-cylinder engine produced a healthy 130bhp and it had good quality cycle parts too. TRIUMPH

itself admitted, the reigning Honda CBR900RR FireBlade and Ducati 916.

"We were chasing [the FireBlade market] with this bike," Triumph's Miles Perkins said years later. "It [the T595] was going to be our highest performance motorbike – it was a huge departure for us."

To achieve that performance, in came a (virtually) clean sheet design. Although the three-cylinder engine was an evolution of Triumph's older triples, it lost a hefty 12kg, gained 70cc of swept capacity, added, via assistance from F1 auto-engineering consultants Lotus, an all-new top end with bigger valves and new cams, and adopted an early form of motorcycle fuel-injection, this time from French firm Sagem.

The modular bike's old, top heavy, steel spine frame was also junked in favour of an all-new, oval-section, aluminium perimeter affair designed in collaboration with chassis specialists Harris Performance; a Ducati 916-style single-sided swingarm graced the new bike's rear end, while top-notch cycle parts included Showa suspension, Nissin brakes, and Bridgestone BT56 Battlax tyres.

Finally, bold, curvaceous styling came from renowned British designer John Mockett, the name, T595, was Triumph's internal factory codename but added to Triumph's traditional 'Daytona' sports bike moniker, and

the result, with a claimed 130bhp, was pretty much on par for the class, while having a distinctive, three-cylinder character all its own.

The T595 Daytona was a big success, too, becoming a UK best seller – at least at first, anyway. But despite making a big initial impact, magazine comparison tests soon revealed that, although good, the T595 neither had the power nor light weight to beat its intended competition; there were problems with the ambitious fuel injection system, the T595 moniker proved problematic (some assumed it was a 600cc machine) and, worst of all, not long after its launch, reports of the frame cracking near the headstock led to an expensive recall to have them all replaced.

With hindsight, the Daytona never truly recovered. Rectified bikes had silver painted (rather than polished) frames to set them apart. In 1999 an updated Daytona 955i replaced the T595 and in 2001 it gained a power boost to a claimed 149bhp, lost 3kg thanks mostly to a more conventional, twin-sided rear swingarm (a change which was later reversed) and the styling was updated, too – even though some thought it was for the worse.

But, despite being a much better bike, at least dynamically, it was also all too little and too late. Those later 955is lacked the 'wow' factor, certainly in terms of looks, of the early Daytona while, with the arrival of the 1998 Yamaha R1 and 2000 Suzuki GSX-R1000, the world had moved on in terms of performance. For its final few years the Daytona drifted on as a road sports tourer

more akin to Yamaha's Thunderace than a true superbike and the model was dropped entirely in 2006, never to return, not in true 1000cc superbike form anyway.

That's not the end of the story, however. Although initially conceived alone, the success of the earlier 1994 Speed Triple 900 inspired a new naked version, the T509 Speed Triple, to be launched alongside.

"There wasn't always going to be a Speed Triple," admitted Triumph's Stuart Wood years later. "But very soon after we started the project, we decided there was going to be a Speed Triple version."

That bike was even more successful than the Daytona, something that surprised even Triumph itself. Although the Daytona was initially the better seller, the Speed Triple slowly grew in stature then began outselling its stablemate.

"At launch, we wouldn't have expected it to outsell the Daytona, not at all," remembered Wood. "The Daytona initially, actually, was huge. Absolutely huge – because that was where the market was: in faired bikes. But very quickly people realised this naked bike, with this style and aggression, was a very cool thing and it just grew and grew and grew and overtook the Daytona."

Today, the Speed Triple, four generations on, remains the definitive Triumph and the backbone of the British brand's range. But it would never have happened without the T595 Daytona superbike, a machine which, increasingly, is viewed as a modern classic. ■

> **66 *It was a big success, too – at least at first, anyway* 99**

1998 APRILIA
RSV MILLE

The Italian lightweight specialists go big with their first V-twin superbike

By 1995, lightweight specialists Aprilia were probably the most dynamic and ambitious Italian motorcycle manufacturer of all. Its racy 125s were dominating the quarter-litre class, its recent RS250 was the best of its type, and in smaller racing classes it was sweeping all before it. The firm's aim was to become Europe's biggest manufacturer – the Italian Honda – and only a rapid expansion of models on top of the marque's traditional 125 and 250 two-stroke offerings would achieve that. Now was its time to 'go big'.

As charismatic Aprilia CEO and driving force Ivano Beggio said

years later: "Ducati, with their 916, were selling a lot, as well as all other Japanese bikes, and so, in 1998, Aprilia had to enter the market. But because the Ducati was very elegant and refined, we felt we had to be more masculine, more powerful – reliable but tough. A thoroughbred."

The result was not only the first Aprilia superbike – the 1998 RSV Mille, with its sights set firmly on the 916 – but also a selection of variants topped off by a homologation special aimed at world superbike racing success. The new bike's 'heart', meanwhile, an all-new 998cc V-twin produced by Austrian partner Rotax (as were nearly all Aprilia

engines up to that point), would also form the basis of a new family of big-bore Aprilia V-twins including sports tourer, half-faired street sportster, and adventure bike.

On paper, the Mille seemed to have it all. Its 60° V-twin produced a 916-beating 128bhp, its exquisite, polished, aluminium twin spar frame was a work of art and held top spec cycle parts including multi-adjustable suspension and Brembo brakes. Its distinctive dash was glorious, and its build quality was excellent, too. And if the Mille's bulbous, quirky styling complete with unique 'three headlight' face, was a little unusual, at least it meant the Mille stood out from the crowd.

ABOVE: You can't fault Aprilia for ambition. Its first big bike was a V-twin superbike designed to take on the then dominant 916 from Italian rivals Ducati.
APRILIA

On the road the Mille had the 916 beats, too, being more flexible, roomier, better equipped, more comfortable and quicker, with 'real world' handling. It worked well on track too, and Aprilia's new big bike also quickly spawned an impressive family of litre-class V-twins, including the SL1000 Falco street sports, RST1000 Futura sports tourer, ETV1000 Caponord adventure bike and, later, the first Tuono super naked.

That first iteration of the Mille spanned five years and three distinctly different models. The base model was updated twice, first in 2001 and again in 2003, receiving increased power, new bodywork, upgraded suspension and brakes, and a host of minor tweaks on both occasions.

More significant, however, were the higher spec R and SP models, the former featuring significantly upgraded suspension, saucier, lighter, Marchesini forged wheels and other performance enhancing extras, with the SP a very limited run homologation-spec superbike with a differently-configured, more powerful engine and, well, more of everything, although only 150 were built and less than 40 made it to the UK.

Beggio added: "I remember our first RSV1000 was nominated Bike of the Year in Germany – in

BELOW: The Mille's 60° V-twin was developed by Austrian firm Rotax. It also had a twin-spar aluminium frame and top-quality cycle parts. APRILIA

SPECIFICATIONS

Price new	£9,449
Engine	998cc liquid-cooled DOHC 60° V-twin
Power	128bhp @ 9,500rpm
Torque	76lb-ft @ 7,250rpm
Frame	Aluminium twin spar
Suspension	43mm inverted telescopic forks (F), monoshock (R)
Brakes	2 x 320mm discs (F), 220mm disc (R)
Tyres	120/70 x 17 (F), 190/50 x 17 (R)
Dry weight	189kg
Top speed	167mph

Germany! And the Tuono which was created from the RSV invented a new segment as a very sporty, powerful naked bike which everyone else copied. They were both a great success..."

American *Cycle World* magazine, in its review in December 1998, said: "Aprilia's RSV Mille has the performance potential to put V-twin sportbikes back atop the heap and do it emphatically. Here is one of those rare serious sportbikes that can do it all – commuter duty, canyon shredder, and sport-tourer – without whupping the rider into submission or forcing him to adapt to various idiosyncrasies."

In truth, and with the benefit of hindsight, both were wide of the mark. The RSV never did quite beat the 916 where it mattered most – on track. The Aprilia's higher centre of gravity and roomier proportions made it more of a handful and, despite the homologation special SP's adjustable frame, Öhlins and shorter stroke engine, it never did claim the WSB crown Aprilia craved.

The 'spin-off' V-twins all had their own problems, often centred around too-rushed development. The Falco, although excellent, had a confused image and proved uncomfortable; the Futura, conceived to be a rival for Honda's all-conquering VFR, had divisive, futuristic angular styling that was at odds with its lumpy V-twin delivery, plus over-soft suspension. The Caponord had suspension problems of its own

and the Tuono, initially launched as a limited edition in 2002, although impressive, arrived too late to make much difference.

By then the RSV had already failed to make the impact intended for it, so a revised, facelifted version went into development – but it was already too late. By 2003, Aprilia was in financial difficulty, stretched further by its misguided purchase of compatriot brands Moto Guzzi and Laverda, and its mostly disastrous entry into MotoGP with its flawed 'Cube' triple, and, in 2004, Aprilia floundered. It was taken over later that year by Italian scooter giant Piaggio which completed the relaunch of the RSV, eventually successfully revitalised both Aprilia and Moto Guzzi (Laverda was shelved) and built the foundations for the all-new V4 RSV which took the superbike world by storm in 2009. That, however, is another story.

Instead, Aprilia's first superbike, although excellent in many ways, must be viewed as something of a commercial failure, setting the company on an over-reaching path that would lead to its demise.

Those first RSVs, due in part to their durability and quality, but also their roominess and practicality, remained brilliant used buys for years to come. They came to be considered as a 'thinking man's Italian superbike', offering great value, and the higher spec R, Factory and SP versions are now highly collectable in their own right. ■

> ## 66 *With the benefit of hindsight both were wide of the mark* 99

1998 YAMAHA R1

Yamaha's own FireBlade-style 'game changer' that revolutionised superbikes

f Honda's 1992 CBR900RR FireBlade rewrote the superbike rule book, emphasising light weight and compactness over raw power, then the 1998 Yamaha R1 proved lightning can strike twice by establishing a new benchmark for power, light weight and control and, in so doing, set the template for all superbikes that followed. Even today, an original R1 is a competitive, credible and impressive superbike.

Although unveiled to a glittering fanfare at the 1997 Milan Show, when factory rider Scott Russell rode the bike on stage wearing a silver suit with a backdrop illuminated only

ABOVE: For its first year, two colour schemes were offered – traditional Yamaha racing red and white, or more subtle and subdued all-blue. YAMAHA

LEFT: 'Move over Honda FireBlade, there's a new king superbike in town.' It didn't happen like that with the Yamaha R1, but that's exactly how it felt. YAMAHA

SPECIFICATIONS

Price new	£9,100
Engine	998cc liquid-cooled DOHC transverse four
Power	150bhp @ 10,000rpm
Torque	79lb-ft @ 8,500rpm
Frame	Aluminium twin spar
Suspension	41mm inverted telescopic forks (F), monoshock (R)
Brakes	2 x 298mm discs (F), 256mm disc (R)
Tyres	120/70 x 17 (F), 190/55 x 17 (R)
Dry weight	175kg
Top speed	1573mph

with the then revolutionary figures of 150bhp and 177kg, the R1's story had begun a full 18 months earlier, at the launch of its predecessor, the YZF1000R Thunderace in January 1996, at Killarney circuit in South Africa. There, Project Leader Kunihiko Miwa, already aware that the 'Ace was too heavy and cumbersome to be a true superbike contender (it was actually pitched as a 'supersport tourer') began sketching out his ideas for a revolutionary new machine.

"In 1991 and 1992 I was working on the development of the YZF750R and YZF1000R ThunderAce, which I was project leader for," he told *MCN* in 2019. "While we were developing these bikes behind the scenes, there was talk about a new machine, a

1000cc inline four that would be the ultimate sportsbike. In 1995 I was asked to become project leader on this new concept, a bike that went on to become the YZF-R1."

He became project leader of not just one new R-series machine but three – the YZF-R1, YZF-R6, and YZF-R7.

All were conceived as 'no compromise' sportsbikes that would bring a new generation of excitement to customers through light weight and high power, and to develop them, Miwa set up three separate design teams as he felt the competition would help development.

It worked, too, as not only did the first, the R1, change the face of sportsbikes, the 1999 YZF-R6 decimated supersports, while the 1999 R7 became regarded as the

RIGHT: At its heart was an all-new, powerful and ultracompact (largely due to its novel 'stacked' gearbox) four-cylinder motor with five valves per cylinder. YAMAHA

ABOVE: The compact engine allowed for a low, forward centre of gravity and for a longer than usual swingarm which also improved handling. YAMAHA

most advanced production bike from the golden era of WSB. Miwa himself, meanwhile, became known as 'Mr No Compromise'.

"We needed to reinvent Yamaha's large capacity motorcycle to allow riders to explore the cornering potential of a bike," Miwa told *MCN* in 2019. When we tested the FireBlade we all agreed the engine wasn't strong enough, but its lack of weight was very good. To prove the point our testing staff created a one-off model to test how much power we needed and what weight the R1 should be. We took a ThunderAce, got it down to 180kg and the test riders reported the weight felt right. So, a target of 180kg and 150bhp was set – which is when the hard work started."

Miwa-san had another target that was arguably still more significant for the R1's success. He knew the new bike had to be far more compact and agile than the EXUP or the

BELOW RIGHT: The genius project leader behind it was Kunihiko Miwa, formerly of Yamaha's 500GP project and later behind the R6, R7, and more. YAMAHA

'Ace in terms of engine dimensions, wheelbase and total width. The success of the lightweight Blade proved 1990s' European sportsbike customers still favoured purity of purpose over compromise, and in particular showed how making big horsepower wasn't enough on its own. The new Yamaha would have to be a radically compact package. And this presented more of a challenge.

One key solution, derived from Miwa's experiences in 500 GPs, was for a 'stacked' gearbox which allowed the engine to be unusually short and kept the centre of gravity (CG) in its optimal position – one problem of the earlier FZ750, for example, had been that its forward inclined cylinder block had moved the crank and thus CG back, away from the front wheel. This in turn unlocked lots of fresh chassis design possibilities. It allowed a short wheelbase for nimble handling but also a long swingarm (copying Yamaha's YZR500 GP bike design), to help stability and prevent wheelies. It would also mean more room to fit suspension, more control over the chain run and associated forces, better control over traction, and greater stability.

The new R1 engine wasn't just shorter; it was narrower too – all drives came off the end of the crank, and plated bores were used instead of liners, saving weight and closing up the cylinders. Its width was reduced further still by fairly conservative bore dimensions: at 74 x 58mm, the R1's bore was narrower than the Thunderace's, which potentially limited the valve area, lowered piston speeds, and could have led to lower peak power

(if not less peak torque) than the older motor. But a reduction in weight (of around 9.5kg on the Thunderace) and less internal friction – including introducing holes between the cylinders to equalise under piston pumping forces (traditionally something Suzuki would bang on about in their GSX-Rs) – meant the R1 motor hung on to its EXUP-valve augmented peak power and torque figures to produce 140bhp at the back wheel – comfortably ahead of its rivals by almost 20bhp and 10bhp up on the Thunderace.

And the R1 was light too – with the engine, designed to be stiff as well light – acting as a genuine stressed frame member, the actual frame itself could be lighter. The result added up to a bike that was 6kg lighter than the rival FireBlade and 11kg down on Kawasaki's ZX-9R, 10mm shorter, had more power than both. At the R1's track ▶

press launch in Spain it simply blew everyone away. *Bike* magazine's then tester Olly Duke, for example, reported: "I'm really worked up, because I've just spent a day at the incredibly twisty Cartagena circuit with the R1. This is the first day of the bike's Spanish launch and I have to say the R1 is everything it's been cracked up to be. And better."

From there the R1 ruled the roost for the rest of the decade so claiming the crown as the ultimate sports bike of the 1990s, Miwa followed it up in 1999 with an equally radical 'little brother', the 600cc R6, which proved just as revolutionary in the supersports class, and the R1 itself wasn't seriously challenged until the first GSX-R1000 arrived in 2001.

Even then that wasn't the end of the R1 story – just the beginning.

In its first update in 2000 the R1 gained over 150 modifications aimed at taming the beast. After launching the bike, Yamaha had discovered that the two-wheeled world wasn't quite ready for a bike as violent as the 1998 model, so it needed a bit of restraint.

The carborettor settings received a tweak, the engine had its friction losses reduced, the gearbox was improved and the R1 shed a further 2kg in weight. The chassis was modified, too, with the bottom yoke stiffened up, weight bias shifted forward, and suspension overhauled, transforming the R1 from a slap-happy animal to a slightly less slap-happy one.

For 2002 the third generation R1 gained a clever fuel injection system and updated (now black) Deltabox chassis, creating one of the most neutral and sweet handling R1s to date. The engine's position within the frame was altered, the trail increased, and the suspension overhauled. Sadly for Yamaha, Suzuki had released the first GSX-R1000 and the sports bike world now wanted thrills rather than refinement...

While in 2004, with the litre class superbikes now dominating the headlines, Yamaha went back to the drawing board for its fourth update of the R1 and completely re-invented the bike, in the process creating arguably the most beautiful Japanese superbike so far.

Following the then fashion, Yamaha's flagship gained under-seat exhausts, radial brakes and even had projector lights. But there was even bigger news with its engine. Claiming 172bhp from a brand-new big bore/short stroke 998cc inline four with the firm's traditional five-valve head design, the 2004 R1 was the first litre bike to hit the magic 1:1 power to weight ratio thanks to a 172kg dry weight. And when the forced airbox was factored in, Yamaha claimed the R1 actually produced 180bhp! However, there was a problem: the R1 just wasn't

exciting, and the motor was so tall geared it felt flat and lethargic.

Further changes came in 2006, although this generation was more a stop-gap tweak than a major overhaul. In an effort to appease racers, Yamaha improved chassis stiffness, grafted on a 20mm longer swingarm, added 3bhp and a few cosmetic alterations including gold fork legs, but if you weren't a world class racer, you probably wouldn't have noticed.

ABOVE: The 1998 Yamaha R1's part LCD digital, part analogue dash was another world first. YAMAHA

RIGHT: Today, the original 1998 R1 (especially in red and white) remains one of the most distinctive, successful and desirable superbikes of all. YAMAHA

LEFT: The result was officially unveiled at EICMA in Milan in November 1997, ridden on stage by no less than factory WSB star Scott Russell. YAMAHA

In 2007 Yamaha took the radical step of abandoning its by-then traditional five-valve head in favour of a more conventional four-valve design – and that was just the start. The 2007 R1 was also the first litre bike to gain a 'ride-by-wire' throttle (the R6 was the first bike to get this in 2006) and the first production motorcycle to have variable length intake funnels, a system that was meant to boost the R1's bottom end while also helping it breathe high up in the revs. Unfortunately, that also meant that it lacked the bottom end riders expected from a litre bike and was frustrating at low revs. The R1 needed a unique selling point, something Yamaha gave it two years later...

The 2009 Yamaha R1 was arguably the most significant litre class superbike since the original in 1998 – YZF-R1 – which was entirely down to one reason: its 'crossplane' crankshaft.

Developed on Yamaha's MotoGP winning M1 race bike, the crossplane crank was claimed to help reduce inertial torque. Where a conventional inline four's pistons move in pairs, the crossplane's pistons are spaced unevenly, creating a unique 'long band' firing order. The theory was that, as the R1's pistons weren't ever all stationary at the same point as they are on a conventional inline

four, the crossplane smoothed out the power delivery, improving drive out of corners.

It worked, too – and sounded like nothing else, with the result that Yamaha's four-stroke engine design philosophy was changed forever, with crossplane engines still forming the bulk of Yamaha's 'MT' family to this day.

That success was also helped in no small part by American rider Ben Spies taking the firm's first WSB title that year.

However, with 2009 also seeing the arrival of Aprilia's all-new RSV4, and 2010 the introduction of BMW's brutally powerful (and sophisticated) all-new S1000RR (in turn followed by an even more electronics-laden RSV4 in 2011), the crossplane R1's reign was short.

Sadly, due to the 2009 global financial crisis effectively putting the brakes on the development of the Japanese motorcycle market, Yamaha's backs were up against the

wall, and it was a few years before Yamaha was able to fight back.

In 2012 a mildly updated R1 featured the firm's first sportsbike traction control system and not a lot else, aside from new footpegs, ECU tweaks and nose.

Finally, in 2015, Yamaha unveiled another all-new YZF-R1 – a machine that would prove to be the last of an amazing dynasty of superbikes.

Drawing even more heavily from its M1 MotoGP machine, the 2015 R1 took Yamaha into the 200bhp club along with the most sophisticated electronics suite yet seen on a road bike. There was also a limited run R1M, which featured semi-electronic Öhlins suspension, carbon fibre bodywork, and even more electronic wizardry.

A further revision came in 2020, principally to meet the latest emissions regulations, and it is this version that enjoyed a clean sweep in the major superbike championships in 2021, powering Turkish Toprak Razgatlioglu to the world title, Brit Tarran Mackenzie to the British series, Jake Gagne in MotoAmerica and Katsuyuki Nagasuga in Japan.

The R1 had finally returned to superbike dominance but it's the 1998 original that is still considered as one of the most collectable of all modern superbikes. ∎

1999 MV AGUSTA 750 F4

A legend is reborn with one of the most mouthwatering superbikes of all time

I f there was a prize for the most exotic, beautiful, exclusive and desirable superbike of the 1990s, the F4 750 would surely win it hands down.

Which isn't at all bad for a machine which was also demonstrably, right from the outset, a long way from also being the best.

The dream project of the family business that had earlier rescued Ducati, styled by the design genius who also came up with the Ducati 916, and bearing the most revered name in Italian motorcycling history, the first bike of the revived MV Agusta concern had it all – or rather, it nearly did.

After buying and reviving Ducati in the late 1980s and early 1990s with models like the 851, Monster and 916, Claudio Castiglioni's Cagiva concern surprisingly sold the Bologna marque in 1996 to American investment bank Texas Pacific Group. But what many didn't know at the time was that he had also already quietly bought up the rights to the historic, defunct MV Agusta brand in 1991 and now had even bigger ambitions.

MV Agusta is one of the most fabled, prized, luxurious and sportingly successful motorcycle marques of all. Dormant since the late 1970s, it originally rose to prominence when founded by Count Dominico Agusta as an offshoot of the MV Agusta aircraft company in 1945. In the 1950s it began a long era of racing success with its 500cc four-stroke fours, and between 1952 and 1975 it claimed an unmatched 75 GP world titles, particularly in the premier 500cc class, with an unprecedented 18 world championships for legendary riders such as John Surtees, Mike Hailwood and, most of all, Giacomo Agostini. However, its last GP win came in 1976, its four stroke now outpaced by a new breed of two stroke 500s, and by the decade's end road bike production had been halted, too.

In 1991, however, Castiglioni successfully purchased the brand and funded by the sale of Ducati, aided by the design genius of Massimo Tamburini (who'd earlier designed the Ducati 916) and with the assistance of Ferrari which helped design an all-new MV four-cylinder engine, set out on arguably the greatest of all motorcycling revivals.

The 1999 F4 750 was the result and was – almost – one of the most astonishing superbikes ever built.

ABOVE: It was conceived by MV Agusta owner Claudio Castiglioni and shared some of that bike's signatures such as under-seat exhausts and single-sided swing arm, but with four-cylinder power. MV AGUSTA

BELOW: The original limited edition 'Serie Oro' even had gold-anodised parts, uprated cycle parts and was individually numbered. MV AGUSTA

SPECIFICATIONS

Price new	£11,900
Engine	749cc liquid cooled DOHC transverse four
Power	126bhp @ 13,000rpm
Torque	48lb-ft @ 10,800rpm
Frame	Tubular steel trellis/aluminium
Suspension	49mm inverted telescopic forks (F), monoshock (R)
Brakes	2 x 310mm discs (F), 240mm disc (R)
Tyres	120/65 x 17 (F), 190/55 x 17 (R)
Dry weight	190kg
Top speed	168mph

On paper it had everything: that 'Ferrari' engine, the best cycle parts money could buy and, most glorious of all, Tamburini's styling including stacked headlights, unbelievably narrow flanks, quick-release fasteners, lovingly crafted alloy controls, another single-sided swing arm and no less than four under-seat exhausts, and made every other four-cylinder superbike look clumsy, overweight and basic. Classic MV colours of red and silver were the finishing touch.

Technically, it impressed, too. Fuel injected, compact and with a race-style cassette gearbox, the oversquare four had a voracious appetite for revs and a wailing top-end rush. The frame was a mouthwatering composite of chromoly tubes and substantial alloy side plates, the swing-arm was a work of art, and even the front brakes had six pistons in each caliper.

Later, the great man admitted the F4 was his favourite, too.

"As a complete project the F4 is my favourite," Tamburini said in his later years. "With the Ducati we already had a good base to work on, with the MV it was a blank piece of paper, and we had to create everything, even the smallest of details such as the footpegs. But working on the Ducati was better as it is a cleaner bike when it comes to design; it is far easier to work on, to take apart."

He added: "When you start a project you don't think it could change the course of motorcycle design. I had a lot of luck with the 916: the motor was strong, the company had a good name, and the racetrack success was sensational. But with the F4 it was harder. Right after the launch the company had a crisis, they were unsure if they could make the F4, then the motor had problems as it wasn't powerful enough, but in the end it turned out OK." We'd humbly suggest

RIGHT: Arguably the most beautiful superbike of the 20th century, the F4 had it all: heritage, looks, performance, innovative design... MV AGUSTA

BELOW: Although exquisite, it was delayed, quickly overpowered (by Suzuki's SRAD and Yamaha's R1), and was never a success on track. MV AGUSTA

"OK" may be understating it slightly, but as he suggests, that 126bhp wasn't quite enough

Production delays had meant that by the time the F4 came to market, Suzuki's 128bhp GSX-R750 SRAD and Yamaha's more powerful (and lighter) R1, outperformed the F4 even before it had been launched. And although it handled well and was desirable, the F4 was also prohibitively expensive; it was heavy, Cagiva's MV dealer network was insufficient, and there were other teething troubles, too, all of which devastated Castiglioni's MV dream.

The F4 got better – evolving into a 1000 in the early noughties – and revived MV survived – just. A naked roadster version, the Brutale, followed and had an appeal all its own, while a smaller, three-cylinder F3 also had an impact, but problems were never far away, and neither MV nor the F4 ever achieved the street or race success originally hoped for.

By the late noughties MV was again in financial trouble, leading to a short lived, also failed

takeover by Harley-Davidson. That lasted just two years and cost the American giant millions before it was infamously sold back to Castiglioni for just one Euro. But at least the brief marriage paid for the creation of a second generation F4, this time styled by Brit Adrian Morton, which lived on for a further decade, although that variant has never been as fondly remembered as the original.

The 1999 original, as an example of 'motorcycle made art' and as an ultra-desirable modern classic, the F4 750, especially in launch 'Serie Oro' top spec limited-edition trim (of which just 300 were made), remains one of the most iconic superbikes of all time. ■

1999 YAMAHA R7

Yamaha's beautiful homologation special racer... that never quite delivered

Almost... but not quite. Yamaha's 1999 R7 homologation special racer was built to win the world superbike championship and has another internal designation that tells you all you need to know about the last, and one of the greatest 750cc superbikes of the 1990s – OW-02, the successor to the OW-01.

It combined everything Yamaha knew about four-cylinder performance, blended it with the best components available, and was wrapped in arguably the most beautiful Japanese sports bike bodywork ever.

The result had a five-valve, 749cc four capable of 160bhp, a bespoke aluminium Deltabox frame with adjustable everything; top-spec, multi-adjustable Öhlins forks and rear shock, while lightweight wheels and tank added up to a dry weight of just 176kg. It was also the rarest homologation special Japanese superbike of all. Just 500 were built (the minimum required to qualify) and sadly, due to its comparative failure, its lifespan was painfully short.

The reason for that failure is quite simple. As a four cylinder, under then WSB regulations, the R7 was limited to 750cc when the competing V-twins, most obviously Ducati's dominant 916/996/998, could have a full 1000cc, a potential power discrepancy, as Honda had already

ABOVE: Is this the best-looking Japanese superbike ever? Many think so. Unfortunately, the Yamaha R7 (also known as OW-02) wasn't a success on track. YAMAHA

discovered with its RC45, and the Yamaha was unable to make up.

A second problem for the R7 was that it was built in one form which produced just 106bhp. That was due to a combination of its limited numbers making just one version viable, which then prompted Yamaha to defer to the then German-required spec of 106bhp. Of course, that wasn't the overall intent. Although sold, necessarily, as a road legal machine, a sophisticated race kit was also available (but only to genuine racers) which comprised: new wiring loom, head gasket kit, race spec spark plugs, high-flow fuel pump and regulator, airbox kit, radiator, exhaust and so on which, together, boosted power by a whopping 55bhp and price by a further £10K.

But that price also gives a hint to the R7's final problem. Even in stock road trim it cost £22,000, with the kitted racer well over £30K. But as a racer, because of the capacity disparity, it still wasn't competitive and, as a road bike, its rarity, price and power (that 106bhp was a full 14 less than the then road-going R6 supersport, at about a third of the price) made no sense, either.

And yet... the R7 was still some kind of ultimate. Gorgeous, super-fine handling, beautifully made and exclusive, the R7 remains still, arguably the ultimate incarnation of the Japanese 750cc four-cylinder superbike and one of the rarest machines of the 1990s. Even if it never did win the world superbike crown, it was designed to deliver. ■

SPECIFICATIONS

Price new	£22,000
Engine	749cc liquid-cooled DOHC five-valve transverse four
Power	106bhp @ 11,000rpm
Torque	53lb-ft @ 9,000rpm
Frame	Aluminium twin spar
Suspension	43mm inverted telescopic forks (F), monoshock (R)
Brakes	2 x 320mm discs (F), 245mm disc (R)
Tyres	120/70 x 17 (F), 180/55 x 17 (R)
Dry weight	176kg
Top speed	174mph

LEFT: Although fine-handling and gorgeously built, like the RC45, it was also underpowered in street form and, again, prohibitively expensive. YAMAHA

2001 SUZUKI GSX-R1000K1

Suzuki returns to superbike dominance with a 1000cc beast

SPECIFICATIONS	
Price new	£8,999
Engine	988cc liquid-cooled DOHC transverse four
Power	160bhp @ 10,500rpm
Torque	76lb-ft @ 8,250rpm
Frame	Aluminium twin spar
Suspension	43mm inverted telescopic forks (F), monoshock (R)
Brakes	2 x 320mm discs (F), 240mm disc (R)
Tyres	120/70 x 17 (F), 190/50 x 17 (R)
Dry weight	170kg
Top speed	181mph

ABOVE: After the GSX-R750WT, Suzuki followed with a 600, then 1000cc version, which arrived in 2001. The result, the K1, was the instant new superbike king. SUZUKI

On face value, the 2001 GSX-R1000K1 was 'only' a 1000cc version of the all-new, aluminium beam-framed GSX-R750WT (or SRAD, as it's better known) as introduced in 1996.

In reality, and in terms of its significance, it was more — much more.

After Yamaha redesigned the sports bike 'blueprint' with the 1998 YZF-R1, it was going to take something pretty special from Suzuki to move the game on another giant leap — but that's exactly what the original GSX-R1000 did.

In simple terms, the new GSX-R1000 — a replacement for the old, obsolete GSX-R1100 — replicated what the R1 delivered and added more.

Although its enlarged, 750-derived engine boasted a slightly odd 988cc, courtesy of a bigger bore, shorter stroke, and the addition of fuel injection and a new, gear-driven counter balancer, it evidently demonstrated Suzuki's ability to squeeze power out of a fairly conventional motor by producing a whopping 160bhp — a full 10bhp more than the R1.

And although the new 'Gixxer's chassis was also fairly conventional, in being a beefed-up version of the GSX-R750's beam frame but with Kayaba suspension instead of the 750's Showa units, it managed to be both strong and, crucially, light. At 170kg dry, it was 5kg lighter than the R1, too.

It was all enough for the new GSX-R to overnight, become new 'top dog' in the superbike class. And, if it didn't look too different from the 750, the 1000's mouth-watering gold nitrided fork legs and massive six-piston Tokico brake calipers, were just enough to set it apart. Other detail differences, meanwhile, included a standard steering damper (which it needed) and beefed up, braced swing arm.

The K1 also proved an immediate winner on track, too — well, almost. With the 2001 TT cancelled due to foot and mouth disease restrictions and superbikes still restricted to 750cc fours, the new Gixxer had to wait until 2002 to dominate the TT, something it did again in 2003.

But in 2004, the big GSX-R1000's successor, the K3, won first time out in the British superbike championship (via John Reynolds). It also won in the British Superstock and German superbike championships, and followed them all by Troy Corser repeating the feat in 2005 on the world superbike stage.

And that, really, was the point with the new, 1000cc version of Suzuki's GSX-R superbike. It may not have done anything different, design-wise — or even looked much different. But with clever engineering it set the new class standard, by being a new, class-leading variant of the GSX-R, it re-established the Gixxer as a superbike family par excellence, and by being simply so damn good it provided the foundation for a new era of GSX-R supremacy that would last for more than a decade. ∎

RIGHT: Although no one aspect was pioneering, the GSX-RK1 was more powerful and lighter than the then R1 and the immediate go-to bike for production racers. SUZUKI

2003 DUCATI 999

How do you follow a superbike like the 916? With difficulty...

ABOVE: As the replacement for the 916, Ducati's new 999 had big boots to fill. Although successful, however, it never won the popular vote. DUCATI

Few superbikes in modern motorcycling history have been as controversial or as short-lived as the Ducati 999. It also remains under-appreciated as one of the most pioneering and successful bikes of the early noughties.

Launched in 2003 as the successor to the long lived and hugely successful 916/996/998 series as designed by Massimo Tamburini and first launched in 1994, the 999 not only had huge shoes to fill, it had enormous expectations to match, and almost impossible sporting and race goals to beat. And yet, with the benefit of hindsight over the passage of time, the 999 now should be regarded as a true sporting superbike 'great' which stands comparison with any.

With Ducati now under new ownership (Cagiva sold Ducati to the Texas Pacific Group in 1996, the American private equity firm taking full control in 1998), and with the previous driving force of then owner Claudio Castiglioni and Tamburini now focused on their new MV Agusta dreams, Ducati handed its new superbike project to South African designer Pierre Terblanche who'd worked under Tamburini at Ducati but remained in Bologna when the great man moved to MV.

Tasked to "simplify" and faced with the design burden of the 916 series, which by then had been in production for almost a decade and repeatedly updated to the extent that its design now seemed fully exhausted, apart from retaining its tubular steel trellis frame and 90° L-twin engine layout, Terblanche's solution was effectively a clean sheet design.

"Before we even got started on the 999, I had my guys sketch all of the existing sportbikes' front and rear ends... then told them I didn't want to see any of that ever again," he recalled later. Instead, he had them look at pictures of Formula One cars, which ultimately resulted in the 999's smooth-sided fairing and distinctive air conveyers.

So, out went the 916's angular lines and pointed nose, in came controversial curves. Also out were the former's side-by-side twin headlamps in favour of twin, vertically stacked ones, the 916's dual under-seat exhausts (which were replaced by a single unit), and the 916's 'signature' single-sided swinging arm for a more conventional twin-arm unit, which was justified by Terblanche for being both lighter and stronger.

The result, when unveiled towards the end of 2003, caused a sensation – and not for all the right reasons. The 999's new technical advances may have been largely undisputed, but its overall 'aesthetic' proved divisive at best, meeting with criticism from many loyal Ducati fans who had become accustomed to the 916 which by then had often been described as one of the most beautiful motorcycles ever made.

In reality, 'under the skin' the 999 was not just a significant technological step forward, it was also an impressive performer. The updated engine, with revised valves and intakes, and electronics and injection changes, not only gave even more power but added torque, too; the new tubular steel trellis frame delivered improved handling but, crucially, far more

RIGHT: On track it proved very successful, winning numerous superbike championships both on the national and the world stage. DUCATI

adjustability and comfort, with the seat being adjustable laterally to provide extra legroom for taller riders, something the 916 series conspicuously lacked. While the new, strikingly space age-looking single dial dash was another obvious upgrade, at least for many.

As had become the norm with the previous 998 and 996, three versions of the new bike were offered: the standard model, the 999, the uprated 'S', with Öhlins suspension, lightweight forged Marchesini wheels, improved Brembo brakes and 136bhp, and the top specification, more track-orientated 'R' with titanium valves and even more power (139bhp), a magnesium head and cam covers, carbon fibre bodywork and Termignoni race exhaust. The R was launched first and — despite protracted misgivings about its looks — proved the doubters wrong by being an immediate race success.

The factory race version, the F03, dominated that year's world superbike championship like no new bike had before. New British team leader, Neil Hodgson, ably supported by Spanish teammate Rubén Xaus, monopolised the podium at the first race of the season with the Ducati Fila factory team. Aboard his number 100 machine, Hodgson then went on to win 11 of the year's first 12 races, scored two more victories later in the year (along with seven second places), and duly claimed the 2003 World Superbike title with a whopping 489 points.

At the end of the season, the Briton famously drew a red line through the double zero of his race number, thus transforming the 100 used up to that moment into the world champion's number 1.

Hodgson was not the only one to race the 999 to great success. In 2004, with Hodgson having departed to MotoGP, British compatriot James Toseland replaced him in the Ducati works team and promptly took the 999 to another WSB crown. Spaniard Gregorio Lavilla then, in 2005, claimed the British superbike title aboard a factory supported 999, while in 2006 Ducati reclaimed the world crown with the 999 in the hands of multiple champion Troy Bayliss.

Nor did the 999 remain unchanged over that time. In 2005, after just two years, in response to the original's lukewarm reception, the 999 received a significant facelift and power upgrade, featuring a wider, more rounded top fairing and taller screen, a now colour-matched frame, a black exhaust cover, swingarm, and subframe, and an uprated, more powerful 140bhp engine thanks to higher-lift cams, a lighter crank, and a race-style deep oil sump. The base model also gained a WSB-style braced aluminum swingarm, while the 999 S received radial-mount brake calipers for the first time.

Sadly, it still wasn't enough. Ducati pulled the plug on the 999 after 2006 to make way for the more traditionally beautiful 1098 (which also saw the return of the single-sided swing arm), however the 999 remains one of the most pioneering and successful superbikes of modern times. ◼

> **66** *Ducati pulled the plug on the 999 after 2006* **99**

ABOVE: Today, the 999's appeal is growing, especially in its top spec 'R' form with Öhlins suspension, extra power, and Brembo radial brakes. DUCATI

BELOW: Although advanced and, in many ways, a significantly better bike, the 999's Pierre Terblanche styling proved controversial and unpopular. DUCATI

SPECIFICATIONS

Price new	£11,250
Engine	998cc liquid-cooled Desmodromic 90° V-twin
Power	124bhp @ 9,700rpm
Torque	66lb-ft @ 7,800rpm
Frame	Tubular steel trellis
Suspension	43mm inverted telescopic forks (F), monoshock (R)
Brakes	2 x 320mm discs (F), 240mm disc (R)
Tyres	120/70 x 17 (F), 190/50 x 17 (R)
Dry weight	199kg
Top speed	168mph

As the bike that rewrote the 'superbike rules' in 1992 before going on to dominate and be one of the category's best-known models for over 30 years, it's no surprise Honda's Fireblade is featured more than once here. With more than a dozen models over those three decades, we could have included it numerous times. But, after that 1992 original, there's one that stands out.

There's a certain irony that the first Fireblade designed by a team not headed by Tadao Baba, the much-fabled designer behind the original, was also one of the best.

Instead, inspired by Honda's new four-stroke MotoGP racer and now with a full 1000cc, the 2004-2005 Fireblade is considered one of the best all-around superbikes of this era, praised for its balance, predictable power delivery and forgiving chassis.

The 2004 CBR1000RR was a 'first' in many ways. An all-new design, it was the first to be called, not FireBlade, as per all the 'Baba-era' models, but 'Fireblade', as a mark of respect to the great man.

It was the first designed to be competitive in the new 1000cc World Superbike Championship (which, from 2004, shifted from a 750cc/four-cylinder formula to a 1000cc one) and so was far more track orientated than before. And it was also the first to be inspired by, leverage technology from, and even be styled to mimic Honda's then all-conquering RC211V which, by 2004, had already dominated the first two championships of the new four-stroke MotoGP formula.

Other 'firsts' included Honda's first radially mounted brake calipers,

2004 HONDA CBR1000RR FIREBLADE

Honda's Fireblade superbike becomes a replica of its MotoGP wonder...

LEFT: Now called the Fireblade (with small 'b'), the 2004 CBR1000RR was the first to be modelled on Honda's then dominant MotoGP RCV racer. HONDA

being the first 'Blade with fuel injection and the first with an under seat exhaust.

The engine was all-new – not a development of the original 898cc unit – with the more oversquare and compact 998cc four fed transmitting drive via a race-inspired, cassette-type gearbox.

This seventh generation 'Blade's chassis was even more MotoGP-inspired, featuring an all-new die-cast frame, a longer and stiffer 'Unit Pro-Link' swingarm, and a pioneering Honda Electronic Steering Damper (HESD) for improved stability.

The most 'GP-alike' feature of all was its RCV-inspired styling. For the first time it was possible to buy a 1000cc superbike which was 'the spit' of Honda's GP racer. You could even buy one in replica Repsol race livery.

The result was fast, fine handling and yet typically Honda in its refinement and all-round ability, yet some criticised it for almost being bland. It didn't matter. The 2004 Fireblade marked a significantly more advanced, race-orientated direction for Honda's superbike.

An updated version in 2006 was even better (and arguably the best of all the 'analogue' superbikes), and in 2007 it finally achieved its ultimate goal — winning the World Superbike championship in the hands of Brit James Toseland. Superbike measures of success don't get much better than that. ■

BELOW: With its striking 'GP-alike' styling, including under seat exhaust, radial brakes and sharp handling, it was more than enough for any 'wannabe' GP racer. HONDA

SPECIFICATIONS	
Price new	£8,799
Engine	998cc liquid-cooled DOHC transverse four
Power	172bhp @ 11,300rpm
Torque	75lb-ft @ 8,500rpm
Frame	Aluminium twin spar
Suspension	43mm inverted telescopic forks (F), monoshock (R)
Brakes	2 x 310mm discs (F), 220mm disc (R)
Tyres	120/70 x 17 (F), 190/50 x 17 (R)
Dry weight	179kg
Top speed	177mph

2004 KAWASAKI ZX-10R

Kawasaki re-enters the superbike class with the wildest 1000 of all

With the move to full track-inspired superbikes starting with the 1998 Yamaha R1 which was in turn then leapfrogged by the 2001 Suzuki GSX-R1000K1, then joined by the MotoGP/RCV-inspired all-new CBR1000RR Fireblade of 2004, the last of those from the Japanese 'Big Four' was from Kawasaki, also in 2004. And it was probably the wildest, maddest of the bunch.

Kawasaki is arguably the most performance-focused of the Japanese manufacturers, due to both its wild 750 H2 two-stroke then Z1 900 in the 1970s. This element is maintained today by machines like the supercharged Ninja H2, but it hadn't produced a class-leading, pure sports superbike since the 1984 GPz900R Ninja. (Incidentally the Ninja H2 was named in honour of both the '70s two stroke and the '84 GPz.)

That all changed with the 2004 ZX-10R. Inspired by Kawasaki's entry into the now four-stroke MotoGP series and stealing the name (but nothing else) from the 1988 ZX-10

(which was the successor to the 1986 GPZ1000R which in turn followed the 1984 GPz900R), the new ZX-10R C1 Ninja, to give it its full name, was fierce, light, raw and potent, and took the superbike world by storm.

Initially at least, it was a little *too* wild. Its all-new 998cc four produced an arm-ripping 181bhp; its lightweight, compact chassis comprised a narrow, compact aluminum frame and it boasted some of the first radial-mount brakes and, on track, it delivered exceptional handling and among the most potent performance in motorcycling. On the road, however, its sharp steering and over-firm suspension could deliver head-shaking handling, and the new Ninja quickly developed a reputation as a beast suited only to experienced riders.

With multi-adjustable suspension, a steering damper, skilled 'setting-up', and the rear wheel spindle moved to its most rearwards position, it could be sorted, and the first ZX-10R eventually earned respect as the 'connoisseurs' choice'. It also later won 'Best Superbike' from US *Cycle World* magazine and the international Masterbike competition in its debut year.

In terms of mass sales, on top of the fact that it had been the last to market, the damage had already been done and Kawasaki arguably over-reacted by replacing this first ZX-10R C1/2 with the much tamer, ZX-10R D6, as distinguished by an

under-seat exhaust, which quickly earned it the nickname of 'The Wheelbarrow', in 2006.

Even then they didn't get it quite right, the consensus being that the 'beast' had been over-tamed, so Kawasaki tried again with the ZX-10R E8 from 2008, before finally nailing it with another all-new ZX-10R in 2011, a revvy, sophisticated, track-focused machine that delivered the first of seven world superbike crowns in 2013 and formed the basis of the Ninja that's still one of the very best superbikes today.

None of this would have happened without that original 2004 version, which remains a classic, iconic superbike. ■

SPECIFICATIONS

Price new	£8,650
Engine	998cc liquid-cooled DOHC transverse four
Power	181bhp @ 11,700rpm
Torque	76lb-ft @ 9,400rpm
Frame	Aluminium twin spar
Suspension	43mm inverted telescopic forks (F), monoshock (R)
Brakes	2 x 300mm discs (F), 210mm disc (R)
Tyres	120/70 x 17 (F), 190/50 x 17 (R)
Dry weight	170kg
Top speed	180mph

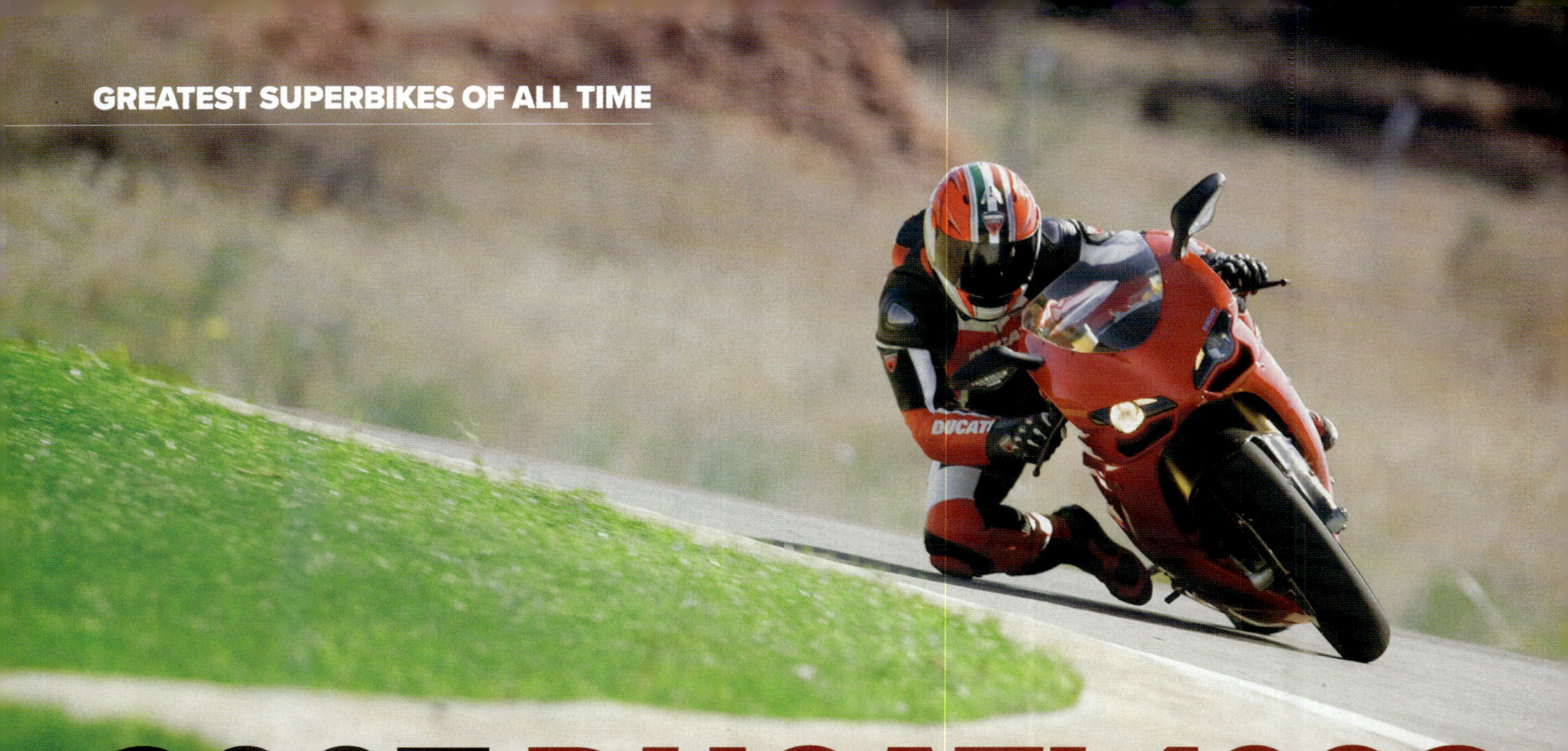

2007 DUCATI 1098

After the flawed 999, Ducati finally gets its superbike right

Ducati's superbike successor to the unloved 999 had but one job: to return the Italian marque to the levels of success – and indeed lust – that had been engendered by the legendary 1994 916. The result, the 1098, pretty much achieved just that. Although still overshadowed by the 916 and ultimately rendered obsolete by its successor, the Panigale, the interim 1098, then succeeding 1198, remains the classic (if not definitive) Ducati superbike.

In simple terms, the 1098 unashamedly regurgitated the 916 styling 'aesthetic', added an updated 'Evoluzione' version of its classic L-twin and, although contrived, executed it all brilliantly, enough to prove a big hit particularly in the important US market and even gaining two more WSB crowns in 2009 and 2011.

Launched in 2007, the development of the 1098 had focused on returning to a classic Ducati superbike outline which again included a single-sided swingarm and under-seat exhausts. It was powered by the new Testastretta Evoluzione L-twin engine and had a more rigid yet lightweight tubular steel trellis frame. Ducati also designed the 1098 to be more approachable, by offering improved handling with a more natural feel than the 999, improving reliability significantly while also, with the 'R' model, introducing the first production motorcycle traction control system.

The Testastretta Evoluzione engine was all-new and marked a significant advance. While retaining the firm's traditional 90° angle, as well as cam belts and Ducati's signature desmodromic valve train system, the rest of the engine was brought bang up to date with more modern engineering techniques, improved tolerances and temperature management, and even a focus on making it easy to

ABOVE: After the poorly received 999, Ducati returned to its traditional values with its successor, the 1098, which was not only fast, but beautiful. DUCATI

SPECIFICATIONS	
Price new	£11,250
Engine	1099cc liquid-cooled Desmodromic 90° V-twin
Power	160bhp @ 9,750rpm
Torque	90lb-ft @ 8,000rpm
Frame	Tubular steel trellis
Suspension	43mm inverted telescopic forks (F), monoshock (R)
Brakes	2 x 330mm discs (F), 245mm disc (R)
Tyres	120/70 x 17 (F), 190/50 x 17 (R)
Dry weight	173kg
Top speed	169mph

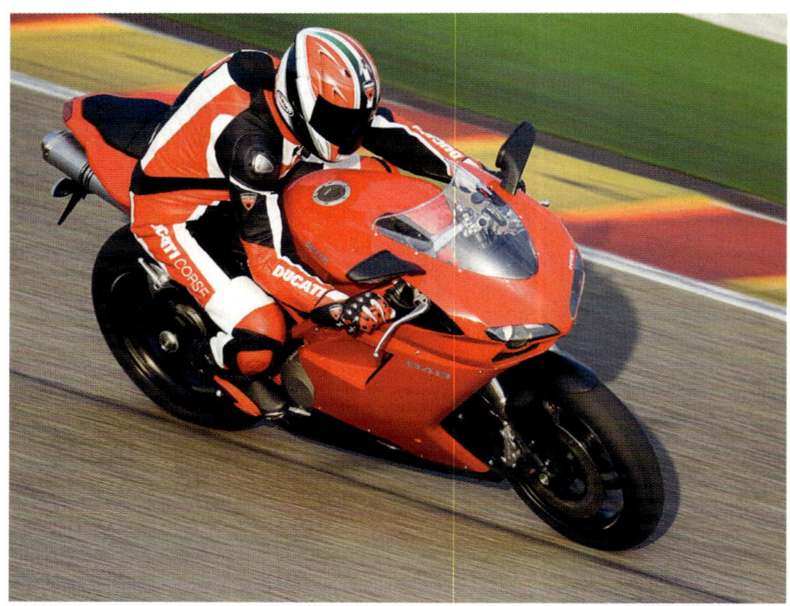

LEFT: As before with the 999 and 916, there was also a junior, more affordable incarnation – the 848. DUCATI

ABOVE: In full race spec, the 1098 also returned Ducati to world superbike winning ways – although it took until 2011 to do so. DUCATI

BELOW: The up-specced 'S' version was the best for the road, but all featured the returning single-sided swing arm and stylish twin under-seat exhaust. DUCATI

maintain. As a result, the 1098 motor is far more robust than those of the previous, ageing 916/996/998 and 999, with much wider service intervals, and most of the older engines' reliability issues removed.

More importantly, with a genuine 144bhp at the rear wheel and 104Nm of torque, the 1098 also managed to not only retain Ducati's traditional V-twin character but did so with more performance than ever.

As previously with the 999, 998 and 996, three versions were offered. The standard 1098 had Showa forks and shock. An up-specced 'S' was given Öhlins suspension front and rear, plus lightweight forged Marchesini wheels (where the base bike has standard alloy items). These changes made the S model 2kg lighter than the base bike, the Öhlins shock was fully rebuildable (where the Showa item wasn't), while its lightweight wheels made the S more agile by reducing its unsprung weight. At launch, the base version cost £11,250 with the higher-spec S version £13,995.

The third version, the range-topping, exclusive track orientated 'R', had a larger 1198cc engine. This featured titanium engine components, more power (180bhp compared to 160bhp of the 1098S), lighter, race-spec suspension including an Öhlins TTX36 rear shock absorber, more advanced electronics, including Ducati's first traction control (DTC – Ducati

Traction Control) and race ECU (Electronic Control Unit), plus Termignoni exhausts and race bodywork, including a single seat.

The result was not just a success in terms of sales but an immediate triumph on track, too, winning the 2008 World Superbike Championship in the hands of Troy Bayliss (giving the Australian his third crown, one each on the factory versions of the 996, 999 and 1098), as well as the British superbike series crown the same year for Shane 'Shakey' Byrne.

It was also just the start of the 1098's significance. As well as putting Ducati back on the superbike map, later that same year (2008), the 1098 spawned Ducati's first superbike-derived 'super naked' when the Italian marque unveiled its original Streetfighter model at EICMA in Milan. Designed by Damien Basset of the Ducati team design, the Streetfighter was based on the 1098 with the same 1099cc liquid-cooled 90° Testastretta engine but produced five fewer horsepower due to a different airbox. In addition to the lack of fairing, the Streetfighter differed from the 1098 bike by having a longer swingarm and therefore longer wheelbase, for added stability, as well as wider handlebars.

Nor did it end there. Having well and truly put the 999 behind them with the 1098, as early as late 2008 Ducati also realised it needed to up its game again to stay ahead of not only a new breed of Japanese inline fours,

such as Yamaha's first 'Crossplane' R1, but increased European competition from Aprilia's imminent RSV4, plus a new V-twin superbike from Austrian brand KTM – the RC8.

Fortunately, Ducati already had the solution. Having been running a bigger capacity version of the Testastretta Evoluzione engine since 2008 in the 1098R, Ducati decided to use a version of this gutsier V-twin in its more mainstream superbikes. Duly, in 2009, the 1098 and 1098S became the 1198 and 1198S.

The result was impressive, producing a genuine 156bhp and 123Nm of torque at the rear wheel, making the 1198 not only the fastest but also arguably the best V-twin superbike Ducati had ever made (even if it was a little intimating for some). Naturally, it was also the most expensive. In 2009 the standard 1198 cost a hefty £12,995, with the higher specced 'S' £16,496. While in R factory race trim, it was also enough to claim yet another WSB title in 2011, this time for Spaniard Carlos Checa.

By then, however, it was also clear that the traditional Ducati L-twin superbike's days were numbered. That 2011 WSB crown would be Ducati's last for many years, with Aprilia's RSV4 then Kawasaki's ZX-10R then dominating for the best part of a decade. Ducati did have in development what it thought would be the solution... but that's another story and in no way should detract from the success of the last of the classic Ducati L-twin superbikes, the 1098. ■

> **" The last of the classic Ducati L-twin superbikes "**

The Desmosedici RR is nothing less than a road-going MotoGP bike with lights.

In 2001 Ducati announced it would be returning to GP racing under the new four-stroke MotoGP formula in 2003. That bike, the Desmosedici, had amazing power and factory rider Loris Capirossi won its first race at the Catalunya GP later that year.

No one, however, predicted what would come next. At World Ducati Week the following May at Misano, Ducati CEO Federico Minoli announced that, in 2006, production of a street version, the Desmosedici RR, would begin.

The result was unveiled at the Italian Grand Prix in 2006, deliveries began the following year and, in total 1,500 were made over the next two years at a price of £40,000 each. The motorcycling world had never seen anything quite like it.

The 200bhp D16-RR (to give it its internal designation) was a replica of the GP6 MotoGP machine ridden by Capirossi and Sete Gibernau in the 2006 championship, with much the same chassis layout, bodywork and 'long bang' 989cc V4 engine architecture.

Many assume the RR owes its existence to MotoGP switching to an 800cc formula in 2007, forcing Ducati to build a completely new race bike and inspiring them to make use of the GP06 by turning it into a road bike. Not so. Instead, a road replica had been part of the plan as far back as 2001 to help finance the MotoGP project and the road-going RR engine was already well into development by 2004, long before the idea of MotoGP dropping to 800cc had even been floated.

Another mistaken belief is that the RR's engine is a carbon copy of that of the MotoGP machine but detuned to lengthen its lifespan and make its performance more accessible, and with an alternator and electric starter. Again, not true. The only parts shared by the two are the cylinder head bolts. Instead, the RR engine was specifically designed to be a road bike and not a modified version of the MotoGP engine.

Even so, the RR powerplant remained a close replica of the

BELOW: With the (carbon) fairing removed, some of the RR's exquisite detailing and sophistication could finally be revealed. DUCATI

2008 DUCATI DESMOSEDICI RR

Is it a superbike? Is it a MotoGP replica? Either way it's a wonder...

Price new	£40,000
Engine	989cc liquid-cooled Desmodromic 90° V4
Power	177bhp @ 13,800rpm
Torque	80lb-ft @ 10,500rpm
Frame	Tubular steel trellis
Suspension	43mm inverted telescopic forks (F), monoshock (R)
Brakes	2 x 330mm discs (F), 240mm disc (R)
Tyres	120/70 x 17 (F), 200/50 x 16 (R)
Dry weight	171kg
Top speed	193mph

GP06 engine, right down to its 'Twin Pulse' firing order. In fact, when the racer switched to this layout in 2004, it forced the RR's engineers to abandon the prototypes already made and follow suit because of Ducati's desire to make the RR as close to its racing sibling as possible.

As such, the RR's engine has the same layout as the GP06 with a 90° V angle, 86 x 42.56mm bore x stroke, 25° included valve angle, and gear-driven desmodromic valves. Many of its components were also from the same suppliers used for the racer. The RR's titanium rods, for example, were by Pankl, as with the MotoGP racer, and had the same journal diameters and eye-to-eye length. The sand-cast crankcases split horizontally just like the MotoGP engine, plus the RR had a replica cassette-type transmission only with beefier gears and shafts.

There were some changes, however. The MotoGP engine used a dry-sump oil lubrication system, but the RR had a conventional wet sump setup as there wasn't enough room for a dry sump system's separate oil tank. Packaging concerns forced the relocation of the water pump from the right side on the racer to the left side below the alternator. While the alternator itself, battery and starter motor also added bulk.

The RR's tubular steel trellis chassis was also necessarily different to the racer's despite again being mistakenly reported to be exactly the same.

While the basic layout was very similar, with a front subframe attaching to the front of the engine along with the aluminum swingarm pivoting directly off the engine cases, subtle changes were made to each to suit the RR's different performance demands.

The RR also permitted Ducati to encourage its suppliers to showcase their strengths. For example, the RR was the first production bike to use Öhlins' GP-spec FG353P gas-pressurised 43mm inverted forks. It was also the first production bike to be equipped as standard with forged magnesium wheels (supplier Marchesini supplied special rims that had been strengthened to suit street use. While even the RR's tyres were 'one-offs', its BT-01R 'Uno' radials developed especially for the RR by Japanese giant Bridgestone.

Some items, however, were more conventional. The RR's LCD instrument panel and mirrors, for example, were basically the same items as used on Ducati's then current superbike, the 1198.

In truth, when deliveries started in early 2008, there was nothing conventional about the Desmosedici RR. Small, compact and firm, its riding position was stretched-out with a long reach to the low-set clip-ons, and its self-supporting carbon-fibre tailpiece had a race bike-style 1in-thick foam seat.

Once started (and the Marelli LCD dash quickly went through a diagnostic check before it did so) the rider was met with a ferocious bark from the dual exhausts. Moving off in first showed the RR to be a little rough before quickly clearing its throat past 3000rpm and revealing a motor with plenty of midrange grunt up to 9500rpm. But past 10,000rpm its power delivery had an intensity like nothing else.

The RR's chassis and handling were truly at another level, and so stiff and focused it made a conventional superbike seem soft — and that's the RR's failing, too. Unless you could ride RR as hard as a MotoGP rider, you'd never get the best out of it. The RR may have been the best handling road motorcycle ever built, but it was an extreme riding experience, only accessible to a very few. As a work of motorcycling art, the RR made everything else seem ordinary. And it still does today. ■

ABOVE RIGHT: Replica Desmosedici RR front, genuine MotoGP Desmosedici 06 behind – there really wasn't that much difference between the two. DUCATI

BELOW: On track there wasn't that much difference between them, either – and yes, that really is world champion Casey Stoner on his race bike in the background. DUCATI

> **66** *Its power delivery had an intensity like nothing else* **99**

f Aprilia's first attempt at a superbike capable of winning the world superbike championship, the 1998 RSV Mille, never quite lived up to expectations, the Italian marque's second, the RSV4 certainly did. In fact, in its top-spec, race homologation factory form, it was not only good enough to win the WSB crown three times; it was so powerful, compact and focused it was likened more to a MotoGP machine. It was a pioneer in electronics such as traction and wheelie control and, although today no longer a WSB contender, the RSV4 lives on, having spawned the Tuono V4 super naked and become the backbone of 21st century Aprilia.

While the original RSV Mille was produced under the regime of founder Ivano Beggio Aprilia, whose big bike ambitions had contributed to the collapse of the company in the early 2000s, its successor was developed under new Piaggio ownership which took over the

Noale concern at the end of 2004.

And where the original RSV had followed the WSB 'model' of a 1000cc V-twin being the template for superbike success, its successor was instead inspired by MotoGP where compact, powerful, 1000cc V4s were becoming the norm. In fact what was to become the RSV4, was originally mooted as a MotoGP bike and, later, its engine would form the basis of its RS-GP MotoGP racer.

The result was the product of a 'brain trust' that included Claudio Lombardi (previously with Ferrari and later associated with the infamous 990cc three-cylinder 'Cube' MotoGP project), Romano Albesiano (later Aprilia Racing technical director), Luigi Dall'Igna (current Ducati Corse general manager) as well as

ABOVE: The RSV4 and Biaggi won again in 2012, while Frenchman Sylvain Guintoli took a third crown for Aprilia in 2014. APRILIA

legendary designer Miguel Galluzzi. It was powered by an all-new 999cc 65° V4 engine (the first production four-cylinder unit made by Aprilia), presented on February 22, 2008, at the International Piaggio Group Convention in Milan, and production started in the same year.

2009 APRILIA
RSV4 FACTORY

Aprilia reinvents its superbike with a V4 engine, electronics and more...

ABOVE: Factory world superbike teammates Max Biaggi and Eugene Laverty were competitive from the outset, with Biaggi winning the crown in its second year. APRILIA

BELOW: In top spec 'Factory' trim, the RSV4 reminded one more of a MotoGP racer than a traditional superbike, with brutal power, compact proportions, and slick electronics.
APRILIA

Aprilia's sporting intentions were clear from the outset. The first model was the top spec RSV4 Factory with Öhlins suspension and Marchesini lightweight forged wheels. Aprilia duly entered the 2009 world superbike championship with a full factory effort headed by former GP star Max Biaggi and, in the RSV4's 'shakedown' year, the Italian won the RSV4's first race at the 10th round in Czechoslovakia. Impressive stuff, even if rivals suggested Aprilia didn't qualify as not enough road bikes had been made to satisfy homologation.

But later that same year, repeating the strategy Aprilia had with its original RSV, a second, more mainstream model, the RSV4 R, became available at £12,999 compared to the Factory's £14,999, a tempting saving considering the spec of bike the buyer would receive.

Both shared the 65° V4, exquisite, compact aluminium twin spar frame and style, but where the Factory's engine had electronically controlled variable inlet stacks producing 185bhp and, in race trim, over 200bhp, the Rs did without and produced 180. Where the Factory had Öhlins suspension and forged wheels, the RSV4 R had fully adjustable Showa forks, and Sachs rear shock and steering damper. The R also had heavier cast instead of forged alloys, which pushed the all-up weight 4kg more than the Factory.

Even so, the R was still a beautifully balanced, technology-packed Italian 'missile'. Monstrously fast, it gave loads of confidence in the corners, had superb ride quality, looked great (especially in its new white livery), sounded even better and was massive fun, even if it was a little too extreme for some and, size wise, cramped for taller riders.

All of that potency, of both models, was confirmed in 2010 when Biaggi claimed the World Superbike Championship Aprilia had craved by winning ten out of the series' 26 races.

That was also just the beginning. In 2011 Aprilia raised the bar again when it launched the SE version of the Factory which was revolutionary for introducing cutting-edge electronic riding aids such as traction, wheelie and launch control, plus an electronic quickshifter. Collectively called the Aprilia Performance Ride Control (APRC) package, it ushered in a new 'electronic' superbike era which quickly filtered down through its rivals. As such, the SE version was a truly ground-breaking machine. It also helped fuel a second World Superbikes Championship for Biaggi in 2012, then a third, this time for Frenchman Sylvain Guintoli, in 2014.

While 2011 also saw the first 'spin-off' RSV4 model, the Tuono V4 super naked, which, with its superbike-winning infrastructure but upright and half-faired ergonomics, immediately became one of the best road sportsters of all.

But those developments and improvements also hinted at the future path for the RSV4. Ever since, Aprilia's V4 has been a triumph of evolution rather than revolution. While larger, better-funded rivals eventually overtook the RSV4 in WSB with a succession of new models, including Yamaha's all-new 2015 R1 and Ducati (following Aprilia's example) producing a V4 Panigale in 2019, Aprilia instead updated its superbike as a superior road (and track day) machine.

In 2016 the RSV4 was offered in two new designations, RSV4 RR and RSV4 RF, both lighter, more powerful, and with improved handling and electronics.

With the Tuono having grown to 1100cc in 2015, the RSV4, in 2019, followed suit, discarding WSB qualification to become a better road bike. In 2021, the Factory version was one of the first to adopt electronic Öhlins suspension. And for 2025, Aprilia's long-lived superbike wonder has been updated again with further improved 'aero' and electronics.

Today, the RSV4 may no longer be a world superbikes contender but it's one of the longest-lived and successful, and remains among the most advanced and effective road superbikes ever built. ■

SPECIFICATIONS

Price new	£14,999
Engine	999.6cc liquid-cooled DOHC 65° V4
Power	185bhp @ 12,000rpm
Torque	85lb-ft @ 10,000rpm
Frame	Aluminium twin spar
Suspension	Inverted telescopic forks (F), monoshock (R)
Brakes	2 x 320mm discs (F), 220mm disc (R)
Tyres	120/70 x 17 (F), 190/55 x 17 (R)
Dry weight	179kg
Top speed	186mph

2010 BMW

BMW enters the superbike world with a 193bhp powerhouse

Powerhouse 'looney bikes' weren't associated with BMW – until the S1000RR. Although the German firm's long history of boxer twins had evolved after the 1980s to include the water-cooled K series, F series singles and twins and more, a four-cylinder superbike simply wasn't something BMW had ever been involved in – until 2010.

SPECIFICATIONS

Price new	£10,950
Engine	999cc liquid-cooled DOHC transverse four
Power	193bhp @ 13,000rpm
Torque	826lb-ft @ 9,750rpm
Frame	Aluminium twin spar
Suspension	43mm inverted telescopic forks (F), monoshock (R)
Brakes	2 x 320mm discs (F), 220mm disc (R)
Tyres	120/70 x 17 (F), 180/55 x 17 (R)
Dry weight	183kg
Top speed	186mph

The historic German company's first venture into modern superbike territory shared similar technology to its established Japanese rivals in that it was a conventional DOHC transverse four with 16 valves, stacked gearbox, twin-beam aluminium frame and so on, but in reality it shocked everyone with its powerhouse performance and sophisticated rider aids, and it revolutionised the category with a monster 190bhp, impressive fuel injection and cutting-edge electronics. It even looked odd, with signature BMW 'asymmetric' styling including a 'face' with different headlights (as per the then GS adventure bike), and different side panel venting on either side.

Buit although impressive performance-wise, conventional technology-wise and an immediate success commercially, the S1000RR's path into production was anything but straightforward and, in truth, almost did not come to fruition at all.

LEFT: Before the S1000RR, historic German marque BMW simply didn't do superbikes but what they came up with blew everyone away. BMW

BELOW: Although the RR's basic configuration was conventional in being a beam-framed transverse four, its execution took power to a new level. BMW

S1000RR

As early as the 1990s, there was a growing interest within BMW to rekindle the German marque's long-neglected racing legacy. In the 1920s and 1930s BMW had had huge success on track, both privately and with its factory-supported teams, most famously with Georg Meier when he won the1939 Senior TT aboard the supercharged 255 'kompressor', in the process becoming the first non-British winner of the event.

The first sign of this new ambition was the emergence of a prototype called the R1, years before Yamaha's famous superbike. Between 1989 and 1992 four prototypes were built to investigate the feasibility of competing in the newly established WSB championship. The ambitious design featured a liquid-cooled 996cc DOHC boxer twin complete with Ducati-style desmodromic valves and showed impressive performance potential, but BMW's then commitment to its traditional boxer engine with shaft final drive compromised its likely success.

Soon after that, BMW returned to sports bikes with its 1998 R1100S, which led to the factory-backed one-make BoxerCup race series which supported selected grand prix. This then led to a series of desirable, limited edition production replicas which ultimately evolved into the 2008 HP2 Sport. By this time, however, BMW had already concluded that

ABOVE: The engine, pictured here with front frame section which also acts as the air intake, was good for a new superbike power benchmark of 193bhp. BMW

BELOW: Its styling caught everyone by surprise, too, in being (like BMW's GS) 'asymmetrical', both with its headlights and side fairing vents. BMW

boxers were not the answer to the superbike question.

Instead, it was the transition of the premier grand prix class from 500cc two strokes to 990cc four strokes to create 'Moto GP' in 2002 that was the real catalyst for the development of BMW's all-new superbike, the machine that would come to be named the S1000RR.

Initially, BMW had set about exploring the feasibility of entering MotoGP with an all-new 1000cc racer that was co-developed with Sauber and spied testing on numerous occasions. Originally a 990cc triple, this prototype underwent numerous revisions, all, like Aprilia's similar 'Cube' triple of the period, drawing inspiration from Formula One. At that time, BMW was active in F1 with a high-revving 3000cc V10. So, just as Aprilia's ill-fated MotoGP machine was essentially a 'third' of Cosworth's F1 V10, the BMW triple was, in simple terms, a 'third' of its own F1 V10.

The trouble was, neither met up to expectations. Aprilia's high revving, complex Cube proved a failure and BMW's version was found to be heavy and sluggish, prompting the company to question the worth of proceeding with its MotoGP ambitions.

To reach a decision, BMW researched public opinion on the pros and cons of entering both MotoGP and WSB, and because of these findings, decided to abandon the GP project and instead focus on developing a road bike that would be eligible for WSB.

So, with a blank sheet of paper but also the experience of the ill-fated GP project to draw on, BMW began by assessing the current superbike environment to decide what direction to go in. And at that moment in time, in the mid 2000s, one bike stood out – Suzuki's 2005 GSX-R1000K5, which had just become the first 1000cc four cylinder (under the new WSB regulations which came into force in 2004) to become world superbike champion in the hands of Australian Troy Corser. Only later did the true significance of Corser's involvement become clear.

Soon after, BMW development riders were spotted testing prototype racers based on Suzuki's GSX-R, some even with their frames modified to accommodate a race version of BMW's idiosyncratic 'Duolever' girder-style front suspension. Although distinctive, the fact that the ultimate production S1000RR used traditional, conventional telescopic forks suggests this system didn't perform as well as hoped…

Later prototypes (by then known as the 'K46') were then spotted disguised in bodywork taken from Yamaha's then R6, convincing some observers that BMW was working on a 600 supersports instead of a 1000cc superbike. (Only later did it transpire that, in tandem with its 1000cc superbike, BMW was, like many manufacturers of the time, developing both 1000 and 600cc versions of its new sports bike, but ultimately abandoned the 600 when that market declined.) Finally, near-production ready prototypes were also spotted, this time in their own, distinctive bodywork.

Duly, towards the end of 2008, what was now known as the S1000RR was first seen in its complete, race-ready form ▶

and painted in BMW's iconic 'Motorsports' colors of white, red and blue. At that time, being a racer without lights, there was no indication of the peculiar, asymmetrical twin headlights that would later define the first-generation production machine.

As such, initially at least, the S1000RR didn't truly stand out as much as many expected. Yes, it was compact and sleek, but it was also in the main following the established Japanese superbike formula that Honda, Yamaha, Suzuki, and Kawasaki had been using for years, just with some European Brembo and Öhlins parts thrown in. By comparison, Aprilia's all-new RSV4, which had been unveiled a few months earlier, seemed far more futuristic and ambitious thanks to the V4 engine and chassis designed by Gigi Dall'Igna.

Instead, the full unveiling came in May 2009 at the Monza WSB round, accompanied by no less than new BMW team riders Troy Corser (see, told you he was significant) and Spaniard Ruben Xaus. This was where the asymmetrical headlights (and side fairing vents) were seen for the first time and where its imminent debut in WSB was announced.

On track at least, the all-new S1000RR initially flattered to deceive. In that first year, while rivals Aprilia scored several podium finishes and a race win with

66 *The full unveiling came in May 2009 at Monza* **99**

ABOVE: The aluminium twin-beam frame, inverted telescopic Sachs forks and Brembo radial-mount brakes, however, were entirely conventional. BMW

returning idol Max Biaggi, BMW's S1000RR's top team of Corser and Xaus seldom cracked the top ten.

On the road, however, and in the hands of the press, the new hugely powerful,190bhp S1000RR proved sensational. "The BMW feels like it could do ten-second quarter miles without breaking a sweat and pass the 'gentleman's agreement' 186mph limit in record time," gushed *MCN* in its launch report from new Portuguese circuit Portimão in November 2009, adding: "Handling in standard trim will make the other manufacturers' wince with embarrassment."

But although impressive and immediately competitive on the road, for its combination of class-leading power, real world ergonomics and premium quality, WSB racing success was slow to come. The big BMW wasn't quite nimble enough to beat the best from Aprilia, Ducati and Kawasaki WSB, and it never really won in BSB either. After winning the crown in only its second full year, 2010, the compact, uncompromised Aprilia RSV4 repeated the trick in 2012 and 2014 with BMW, by contrast, struggling to even secure podiums until Marco Melandri challenged for the title in 2012 (he ended up third, but with six race wins – the highest of anyone that year).

Additional race wins for Melandri and Brit Chaz Davies came in 2013, leading to fourth and fifth in the championship standings, but weren't enough to convince BMW to keep its factory team going into 2014. And although private and satellite S1000RRs were still on the WSB grid, they didn't make a significant impact.

Those race and championship wins would come eventually and, in the meantime, the S1000RR was successively updated and improved to become the benchmark road superbike of the 2010s.

Despite being launched right into the heart of the global financial

crisis when bike sales, and especially those of superbikes, fell off a cliff, prompting the Japanese manufacturers to freeze development, the S1000RR proved a huge sales triumph. BMW's solid reputation for durability and reliability played a role, ensuring good residual values, plus, with low interest rates put in place to tackle the financial downturn, the S1000RR's minimal depreciation resulted in surprisingly budget-friendly monthly PCP payments, even though its list price was higher than many competitors.

BMW also repeatedly updated the S1000RR, adopting increasingly sophisticated electronics and refining the design in a 2012 facelift, introducing the carbon-framed HP4 version in 2013 which also showcased new technology such as semi-active suspension. While in 2015 the S1000RR gained another series of updates, including a modified frame and geometry, along with engine updates and even more electronic improvements.

Then, in 2017, the track-only HP4 Race represented the ultimate incarnation of the first generation S1000RR. With a staggering price of £68,000, the HP4 Race not only boasted the most power yet, at 215hp, but thanks to its full carbon fibre frame, it weighed in at just 146kg dry, with the two providing an experience almost akin to a MotoGP bike.

And although that incarnation effectively marked the end of the first generation of the S1000RR, it also marked the beginning of the second generation one – and the one that would finally deliver the race success BMW sought.

That year, 2017, also saw the first glimpse of its near complete successor, the 2019 S1000RR, and it was every bit as stunning as the original. Officially unveiled in late 2018, the new S1000RR was four years in the making, more

powerful yet lighter, more compact yet roomier for the road, better looking and boasting a raft of new technology headlined by being the first superbike to feature variable valve timing and lift, thanks to the company's ShiftCam technology. Suddenly, even the standard S1000RR boasted power levels that were close to what the HP4 Race had just a couple of years prior (207hp before you even think about aftermarket exhausts), while also meeting future emissions standards.

"The BMW S1000RR is a major departure from the previous model," wrote *MCN*. "Only the name remains the same. Agile, accurate and refined, it handles like a lightweight 600cc supersport racer with the grunt of a V4 and the manic top end power of a competition superbike."

The new S1000RR finally came good on track, too. After a few further years of development and improvement, it spawned the homologations special M1000RR which, in the early 2020s, quickly established itself as the go-to bike for Isle of Man TT racers before, finally, in 2024, and in the hands of Turkish 'wonderkid' Toprak Razgatlioğlu, claimed the WSB crown, quickly repeating the feat the following year.

The S1000RR may have stunned out of the starting blocks with its class-leading power and real roads aplomb, ultimately it also became the class-leading racing superbike, too, whether on road or track. It may have been a long time coming but the S1000RR ultimately proved to be the superbike game-changer BMW had always hoped it would be. ■

The 2012 1199 Panigale was to prove the last 'hurrah' for Ducati's signature V-twin superbike – but what a way to go out!
DUCATI

2012 DUCATI 1199 PANIGALE

Ducati reinvent the V-twin superbike with the astonishing Superquadro

The original Panigale V-twin superbike (as opposed to the current Panigale V4) was launched in 2012 and marked a major change of direction for Ducati. Replacing the 1198 (and previous 1098), the new bike may have followed the Italian company's traditional superbike 'signature' of being a red 'L-twin' but in every other respect it was all new – if not revolutionary.

Unveiled in November 2011 at EICMA in Milan to go on sale early in 2012, Ducati's new superbike not only received a name for the first time (derived from 'Borgo Panigale', the district of Bologna where Ducati is based), in place of its tradition of numbering machines such as the 916, 999, and so on, it had a radically new, short stroke or 'oversquare' V-twin engine called the 'Superquadro' and even dispensed with the marque's traditional tubular steel trellis-style frame in favour of an aluminium monocoque.

At its heart, of course, was the all-new engine. Created to

continue Ducati's V-twin tradition yet designed to compete with the latest generation four-cylinder Japanese (and now German, with BMW) powerhouses in world superbikes, the Superquadro engine was the most extreme V-twin the world had ever seen, primarily due to its exceptionally oversquare dimensions, with a bore-to-stroke ratio of 1.84:1 created to deliver high revs and thus extreme power. In contrast to previous Ducatis, which had belt-driven overhead cams, the new

engine also used gears and a chain. As a result, when launched, Ducati claimed the new 1199 Panigale was the world's most powerful production twin-cylinder motorcycle, producing 195bhp (145kW) at 10,750rpm and 133Nm (98.1lbft) torque at 9000rpm.

And that was just the start. The all-new engine was also designed to serve as a stressed member in the chassis, in turn enabling a radically different frame solution.

LEFT: At its heart was the all-new 'oversquare', high revving 'Superquadro' V-twin, which, capable of 195bhp, was the most powerful V-twin ever!
DUCATI

SPECIFICATIONS

Price new	£14,995
Engine	1199cc liquid-cooled Desmodromic 90° V-twin
Power	195bhp @ 10,750rpm
Torque	97.4lb-ft @ 9,000rpm
Frame	Aluminium monocoque
Suspension	50mm inverted telescopic forks (F), monoshock (R)
Brakes	2 x 330mm discs (F), 245mm disc (R)
Tyres	120/70 x 17 (F), 190/55 x 17 (R)
Dry weight	164kg
Top speed	178.4mph

Out went the traditional, relatively heavy, tubular steel trellis, in came a pioneering (and much lighter) aluminium monocoque, making the Panigale smaller and lighter than a conventionally framed motorcycle.

While another radical feature was the Panigale's exhaust, which was now placed underneath the engine, not beneath the seat as on previous models, which also helped save weight.

The 1199 was also one of the first production sports motorcycles to feature electronically adjustable suspension. Rebound and compression damping was adjusted electronically, while pre-load was still adjusted manually.

As a result, with a claimed dry weight of 164kg (362lb) and kerb weight of 188kg (414lb), Ducati said its 1199 had the highest power-to-weight and torque-to-weight figures of any production motorcycle.

As was by then Ducati's model convention, three variants of the Panigale were offered: the standard 1199 Panigale with Marzocchi forks and Sachs rear shock; the up-specced 1199 Panigale S with Öhlins suspension front and rear, with electronically controlled damping, plus lighter forged wheels. While at the end of 2012, Ducati also unveiled the 1199 Panigale R, a race specification but road legal WSB homologation special with lightened engine internals, including titanium conrods, lowered gearing, a lighter aluminium tank, full Termignoni exhaust, and carbon fibre bodywork. Power was up to 145kW (195bhp) (or 151kW/202bhp) with the track-only exhaust) and weight was down to 364lb (165kg). The S, however, proved the most popular model.

Again, that wasn't the end, as 2013 saw not only an up-specced, limited-edition version, the 1199 Panigale Senna, produced in tribute to the F1 star, it also welcomed the smaller 899 Panigale, in the same way that Ducati had previously produced the 848 (to the 1098), 749 (to the 999), and 748 (to the 916).

While in 2014 Ducati set a new benchmark with the 1199 Superleggera, a special, ultra-exotic version of the 1199 Panigale, designed to reduce weight as far as possible and thus raise performance to a level never seen before. This was achieved through the use of exotic materials such as magnesium (particularly for the monocoque frame), carbon and titanium, which resulted in a dry weight of just 342lb (155kg), and, with engine performance also boosted to over 200bhp, it set a new benchmark in superbike performance – for those that could afford its £70,000-plus price. Just 500 were produced.

But while all these developments amounted to a stunning leap forward over the old, with both revolutionary design advances, searing performance while also being remarkably easy to ride, the new Panigale didn't quite deliver the success Ducati had hoped for.

As a result, the 1199 Panigale was updated in 2015 to become the 1299 Panigale via a capacity increase to 1285cc (the homologation special R remained at the maximum permitted 1199cc). This brought not only increased power and torque but, crucially, also made it easier and less intimidating to ride, thanks to a variety of electronics and geometry updates.

At the same time, in 2015, the 899 was similarly replaced with the new, larger capacity 959 Panigale.

Things improved on track, too. The Panigale finished second in the 2015 world superbike championship in the hands of Chaz Davies who posted five wins. In 2016 the Panigale R won the British superbike championship with rider Shane 'Shakey' Byrne, and the factory supported PBM Be Wiser Team, a feat repeated in 2017 when Davies again came second. And that year, in road racing, Glenn Irwin took his Panigale R to victory in 2017 at the North West 200, also for the PBM Be Wiser team, before winning the Macau Grand Prix later that year.

Yet it still wasn't enough to deliver the WSB crown Ducati so craved, and it was clear that four cylinders would be needed to fend off the threat of the Japanese transverse fours. Fortunately, Ducati was already working on a solution. But the Panigale 1199/1299 was still the most extreme, sophisticated, and potent V-twin superbike ever built. ■

> ## " The most extreme V-twin the world had ever seen "

ABOVE: The driving force behind it was Claudio Domenicali, now the Chief Executive Officer of Ducati. DUCATI

BELOW: Although potent on track, especially after it grew to 1299cc, the Panigale V-twin didn't deliver the world superbike success Ducati sought. DUCATI

2015 KAWASAKI NINJA H2/R

Kawasaki enters the supercharged era with the astonishing 300bhp H2 R

Superbikes simply don't get any more extreme than Kawasaki's sensational, no expense spared H2 R (plus, of course, it's road legal spin-off the H2), the world's first production, road-legal (in the latter's case) supercharged motorcycle.

Look at the numbers. With the R version: 310bhp and a 205mph top speed, plus a 'mere' 200bhp and 201mph for the road legal H2. Look at the style: a supercharged 'Manga' wonder in metallic carbon with influences from past and present, a tubular steel frame blended with a single-sided swing arm, the latest electronics, materials and tech. And just look at the price: £50,000 for the track R, £22K-plus for the 'stocker'. Japanese bikes simply don't get more bonkers!

And yet, strictly speaking, with no racing intent, they're not really superbikes at all…

Instead, both were created simply to be performance icons and new 'halo' machines for the whole of Kawasaki. Inspired and named after two of the Japanese marque's historic milestone machines, the 1971 H2 two-stroke triple and the first Ninja, the 1985 GPz900R, they were created to set a new speed benchmark, with co-operation from across the whole engineering and technology scope of Kawasaki Heavy Industries.

The H2 and H2 R was announced by Kawasaki in a late-2014 teaser campaign following Kawasaki's unveiling of a 1000cc inline-4 with a centrifugal supercharger at the 2013 Tokyo Show.

As for the completed bikes, the H2 R was unveiled first, amid huge media and public interest, at the Intermot motorcycle show in Cologne, Germany, in September 2014, with Kawasaki claiming it could produce 300hp (220 kW), by far the highest rated engine ever for any factory production motorcycle and 50% more than its then nearest rival, the BMW S1000RR. The bike was shown for the first time in North America at the AIMExpo show at Orlando, Florida, in October 2014, which was then followed by an unveiling at the Milan EICMA show in November for its supercharged sibling, the road going H2.

The world press launch for the H2R followed in Qatar in March 2015 and, on all four occasions, the motorcycling world was simply blown away.

SPECIFICATIONS

Price new	£22,000
Engine	998cc liquid-cooled DOHC transverse four, supercharged
Power	200bhp @ 11,000rpm
Torque	98.5lb-ft @ 13,600rpm
Frame	Tubular steel trellis
Suspension	43mm inverted telescopic forks (F), monoshock (R)
Brakes	2 x 330mm discs (F), 250mm disc (R)
Tyres	120/70 x 17 (F), 200/55 x 17 (R)
Dry weight	238kg
Top speed	201mph

BELOW: When Kawasaki launched the supercharged, 300bhp H2 R and road legal H2 in 2015 the world had never seen a superbike like it. KAWASAKI

ABOVE: The road legal H2 'only' came with 200bhp but was also available with a performance exhaust, plus usual road indicators, mirrors and so on. KAWASAKI

BELOW: Stripped of its carbon fibre bodywork, the H2 R reveals a tubular steel trellis frame, race exhaust, single-sided swing arm, and more. KAWASAKI

At the time *Motor Cycle News* wrote: "The H2R you see here is the very pinnacle of what Kawasaki can do … This is the firm's halo product, and every element is Kawasaki at its very best, from the engine and aerodynamic development, through to the mirror-finish black chrome paint specially developed for this model."

Nor was that the end. A sports touring version, the Ninja H2 SX, followed in 2018, with a further variant, the super naked Z H2 in 2020, both having further specification variants of their own. However, as we're dealing primarily with the 'superbikes', here, we'll come back to those later.

All were based around a simply phenomenal, bespoke 998cc four-cylinder motor featuring an entirely in-house designed and manufactured supercharger, although there were significant differences in spec between all models.

The chassis was similar across the H2 range, too, with a tubular steel trellis frame and a single-sided swing-arm (although this was dropped on the 'hyper naked' Z H2), cycle parts were broadly the very best available, including the likes of Brembo radial brakes, while styling wise it has a presence and 'wow' factor like nothing else.

The riding experience, particularly of the R, lived up to that. Although the road-legal Ninja H2 weighed 227kg (501lb) dry and 238kg (525lb) wet (full of liquids and fuel and with tyres), making it no lightweight compared to other superbikes, its whistlingly potent and addictive 150kW (200bhp) delivered a thrilling straight line acceleration rush like nothing else.

Despite its weight, it handled decently, too (although obviously no race-style sports bike) with a classy refinement that comes with being sprinkled with the very best components and design features, including that single-sided swing arm, available.

But the R was something else again, not just due to its extra power, but also thanks to its much lighter weight. In truth, there was much more to the R's differences than that sounds. A big part of the whopping performance increase came from a high-performance exhaust system (with accompanying tune of course) that produced 120dB measured using standard procedures, and was also a big reason for it not being road legal. But, on top of that, many of the engine's internals were also different, with a lower compression ratio of 8.3:1 (against the H2's 8.5:1) yet with higher supercharger pressure 35psi vs 20.5psi for the Ninja H2). The R also had different cam profiles, a different head gasket, different clutch and different ECU mapping tuned for its different camshafts and exhaust. Even the gearing was different, with two fewer rear teeth all in the pursuit of record top speed. In fact, it was reported that the R was built in a special facility off the assembly line, with it taking the plant roughly one business day to produce a single H2R.

Then there was the weight reduction. At 216kg (476lb) against the H2's 238kg (525lb), the R was much lighter than its street cousin due largely to a lighter frame, exhaust and carbon-fibre bodywork but also due to it doing without road legal necessities such as turn signals, mirrors, and even number plate holder.

LEFT: The more extreme (and expensive) R, meanwhile, was only available to a selected few and did without mirrors, indicators, number plate etc. KAWASAKI

BELOW: If you saw this in your mirrors (unlikely, admittedly) it's fair to say you wouldn't be seeing it for long. KAWASAKI

and preparing for four months, a speed of 400kph (250mph) was claimed by a video recording of the bike's dashboard display.

In a sense, of course, none of that really mattered. The Ninja H2 R wasn't road legal, was expensive (initially £41,000, then rising to £50,000), potential customers were vetted, there's no warranty offered (unlike the regular H2), and its exhaust was so noisy that very few circuits would allow it even on track days. As a result, unless you spend all your time riding on runways or intend to tuck it away as a collector's item, there was little you could actually do with an H2 R, and it was difficult to justify. But the

While there were further chassis changes, too. The R's ABS could be disabled; it sported slightly more aggressive geometry via a 50mm shorter wheelbase and minor adjustments to the rake and trail, and it even had bespoke Bridgestone Racing Battlax tyres, which owners were barred from changing to anything else. (Incidentally, other R restrictions included having to apply to buy a bike well in advance as only a few were made each year and having the bike serviced every 15 hours of engine operation above 8000rpm which its TFT dash would log and count down from!)

But, considering the revolutionary, out-of-this-world acceleration and ownership experience the H2 R delivered, none of that really mattered.

"Some will say the H2R's power is too much," wrote *MCN* tester Adam Child at the world press launch in Qatar. "It's too fast, too expensive, too vicious, and yes – it's all those things, but who cares? I wouldn't if I had £50K to spend. Kawasaki promised the H2R would be nothing short of epic and it certainly delivered. It's the ultimate Top Trump card; the fastest, most powerful production bike ever, and it works. Beautifully."

What's more, Kawasaki didn't hold back when it came to underlining and further promoting the H2 (and H2 R's) phenomenal performance.

In June 2015, TT racer James Hillier rode a Kawasaki H2 R around the 37¾-mile TT course on an inter-race demonstration lap at near-race speeds highlighted by a top speed of 'over 206mph' (332km/h) down the flat at Sulby Straight as recorded on Hillier's personal Strava GPS

cyclists' smartphone app, a record for the highest top speed attained by a production motorcycle on the Isle of Man course.

A year later there was more. On June 30, 2016, then five-time world supersport champion Kenan Sofuoğlu, rode a stock H2 R augmented only with special Pirelli tyres (as it was a top speed attempt), race-grade fuel and with Sofuoğlu wearing a special, aerodynamically enhanced, one-piece leather suit, over a bridge in Turkey.

The attempt, with the Turkish president in attendance, was made across the then-newly completed Osman Gazi Bridge, at the time the fourth longest in the world at just over a mile and a half. After training

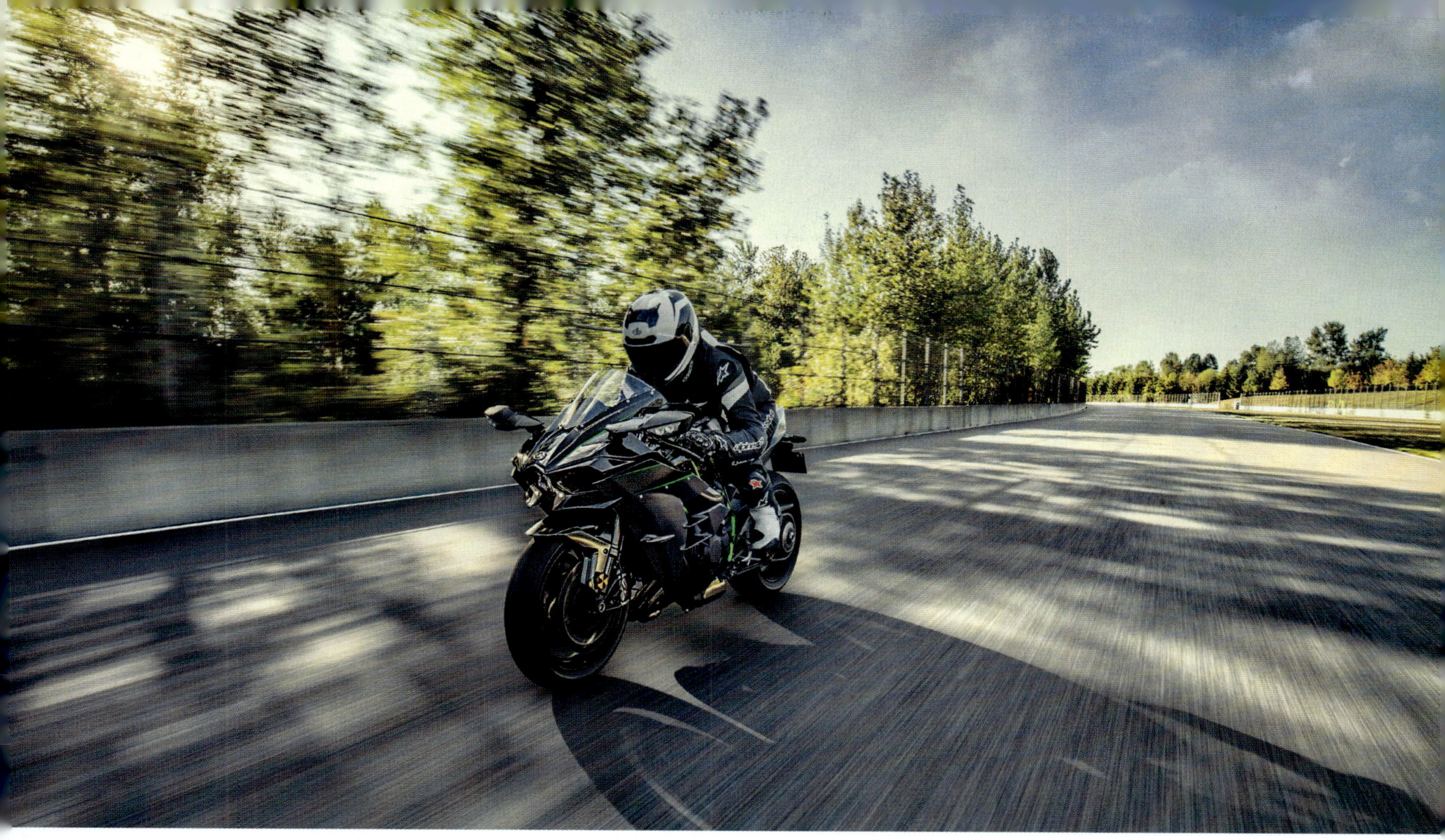

ABOVE: The 'road' H2, meanwhile, was a far more 'civilised' and affordable prospect, if 200bhp and £22,000 can be described as such. KAWASAKI

BELOW: No production superbike has arguably ever been as extreme as the Kawasaki H2 R – or is ever likely to be so again. KAWASAKI

simple fact that it even exists is still phenomenal. Besides, there were plenty of other ways for buyers to enjoy the H2 supercharger thrill (even if diluted slightly).

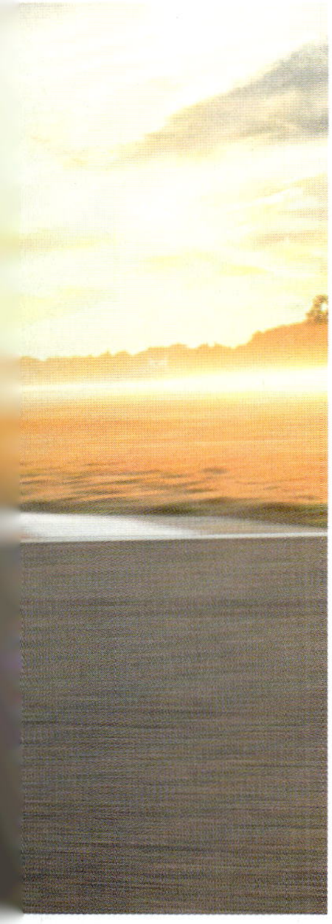

At a far more affordable £22,000, the road-legal Ninja H2 delivered much (but not all) of the supercharged sensation in a far more realistic form. What's more, it came complete with the very latest Akrapovic curved carbon fibre three-dimensional silencer pre-fitted, further enhancing the visual impact and appeal of what is one of the most sought-after motorcycles of 2015.

Later in 2017, a special edition version, the H2 Carbon, was also offered, which, although only slightly different, came with a carbon fibre cowl, a colour change, a numbered stamp and, arguably, more exclusivity than the standard H2.

In 2018 both were joined by an even more 'real world' interpretation, the Ninja H2 SX, which delivered more than a flavour of the supercharged sensation, albeit detuned to 197bhp, but in a more versatile sports-tourer package. This bike was also available in up-specced SE trim (with Öhlins semi-active suspension, full colour TFT dash, uprated electronic rider aids and other detail improvements), and in a variety of 'Packs' ranging from 'Tourer' to 'Performance'.

While in 2020, Kawasaki offered its third supercharged variant, the 'hyper naked' Z H2, with an engine similar to the SX in producing 197bhp, but this time without a fairing and with other chassis revisions including a double-sided swing arm. As was the case with the SX, the Z was offered in two specification variants, the 'base' Z H2 and the up-specced Z H2 SE with Öhlins semi-active suspension, spec and finish upgrades, and more.

Nor did Kawasaki's supercharged wonder end there. Over the course of its life, both the standard H2 and the track-only H2 R received a variety of updates. In 2016, the H2 gained an assist/slipper clutch. The original had been criticised as very heavy,with the new item a claimed 40% lighter with stronger engagement. In 2017 it also gained Kawasaki Cornering Management Function (KCMF) its name for a five-axis Inertial Measurement Unit (IMU) that allowed lean-angle sensitive braking and traction control, while an Öhlins TTX rear mono-shock, improved its rear suspension.

> *"There was little you could actually do with an H2 R"*

In 2019, the H2's power was boosted from 150kW to 170kW (200-228bhp), without ram air, thanks to a revised air filter, intake, spark plugs, and ECU mapping. It also got Bridgestone RS11 tyres, Brembo's new Stylema calipers (which were claimed to have superior cooling to the outgoing Brembo M50 items), and received what Kawasaki called 'self-healing paint'.

The track-only H2 R received similar updates over the same period, namely the slipper/assist clutch in 2016, updated electronics in 2017 via the five-axis Bosch IMU (Kawasaki's KCMF cornering, ABS, and traction control), plus an instrument panel that now displayed lean angle, a new up-and-down quick-shifter, the same new Öhlins TTX shock with remote preload adjustment, but also a different linkage with an updated leverage ratio. While in 2019 the R also got Brembo Stylema calipers, uprated TFT dash with Bluetooth connectivity, and self-healing paint.

For the most part, though, those are mere details. Under it all the H2 and H2 R remain as wild and unmatched as ever. They may have been extreme, expensive and, in many ways, irrelevant, which is why they've also never sold in big numbers, but they also remain unique as modern production supercharged motorcycles, deliver a power thrill no bike can match and, as such are among the most 'super' superbikes of all. ■

2018 DUCATI PANIGALE V4S

Ducati finally discards its V-twin to enter a new superbike era

If the original Panigale, the 1199 of 2012, became known as the ultimate Ducati V-twin superbike, it's successor (while not forgetting the interim, enlarged 2015 1299), the 2019 Panigale V4, was the start of a new era for the legendary Italian brand.

Although the V-twin original, with its oversquare 'Superquadro' V-twin was both a phenomenal performer, incredibly advanced and technologically revolutionary, primarily for its aluminium monocoque frame, its slightly disappointing results on track, especially in world superbikes, underlined the fact that Ducati had

reached the end of the road with its V-twin superbike concept against more powerful V- and transverse fours such as Aprilia's RSV4 and Kawasaki's ZX-10R, which together had dominated world superbike racing since 2012.

Duly, in 2015, with the 1299 V-twin introduced as an interim measure, Ducati began developing an all-new successor and, for inspiration, turned to its MotoGP machine, the Desmosedici.

As its name suggests, the heart of the new bike was an all-new V4 motor, so becoming the company's first production motorcycle to feature a four-cylinder engine in place of Ducati's traditional V-twin, which not only boosted power but gave the exhaust a distinctive new sound.

Initial development started, based

LEFT: After the relative failure, at least on track, of the 1199 Panigale V-twin, it was clear the V-twin had come to the end of the road. The V4's time had come. DUCATI

BELOW: Once again, Ducati's superbike was truly competitive on track, although it took a few years to claim its first WSB crown. DUCATI

SPECIFICATIONS

Price new	£23,895
Engine	1103cc liquid-cooled Desmodromic 90° V4
Power	214bhp @ 13,000rpm
Torque	91.5lb-ft @ 10,000rpm
Frame	Aluminium twin spar
Suspension	Öhlins 43mm inverted telescopic forks (F), Öhlins monoshock (R)
Brakes	2 x 330mm discs (F), 245mm disc (R)
Tyres	120/70 x 17 (F), 200/60 x 17 (R)
Dry weight	173kg
Top speed	191mph

providing a distinct character and sound. It all produced an impressive 214bhp and 91.5lb-ft of torque, making it the most powerful production motorcycle engine in Ducati's history.

Unlike most street bikes and all previous Ducatis (other than its MotoGP racing machines), the Stradale's counter-rotating crank also counteracted the gyroscopic effect of its rotating wheels and therefore decreased the force necessary to change the bike's lean angle.

At the same time, a second version of the Stradale engine, with a smaller displacement to comply with world superbike regulations which prescribed a capacity of 'over 750cc up to 1000cc' for three and four cylinder four-stroke engines, was also developed.

on the 2015 MotoGP racing motor. Ducati said the Panigale V4 was designed to combine racing features, to be competitive in world superbikes, while also being an entertaining and rideable motorcycle with a durable engine. This created the distinct challenge of designing a motor that could not only keep the MotoGP engine's counter-rotating crankshaft and large bore diameter, but also deliver the 24,000km (15,000 miles) service intervals by now expected of a consumer motorcycle.

Called the Stradale, the new V4 road bike motor boasted a swept volume of 1103cc, retained Ducati's traditional desmodromic valves, and had a unique firing order, known as 'Twin Pulse', which mimicked the power delivery of a V-twin, so

RIGHT: The track-orientated R version was more extreme still with an aluminium tank, 'aero' wings, and different spec engine. DUCATI

BELOW: Instead of a true monocoque, as with the V-twin, the Panigale V4 used the engines as a stressed member with two bolt-on subframes and the swing-arm pivoting off the gearbox. DUCATI

Another key innovation was the new Panigale V4's lightweight aluminum perimeter frame in place of the previous Panigale V-twin's aluminium monocoque.

Ducati had reportedly initially been keen to use a development of the MotoGP bike's chassis, again a monocoque, but later changed to a completely new perimeter frame which, the company later claimed, weighed less but offered improved stability and better handling. It also retained Ducati's traditional signature of the single-sided swingarm while being claimed to offer improved control, especially during aggressive cornering. The new bike also came equipped with an updated suite of electronic aids, including a new-generation traction control system, slide control, and wheelie control. ▶

At the same time, the new machine was extensively tested in the wind tunnel in order to maximise its aerodynamic efficiency, both to minimise drag and to enhance stability at high speeds. The resulting machine's sleek lines and aggressive stance were not just for show, they served a functional purpose.

While, finally, although Ducati wanted the performance potential of a MotoGP machine, they also desired it to be accessible and exhilarating for road riders, so paid particular attention to its ergonomics.

It featured the latest generation 5in TFT colour display which integrated via Bluetooth with Ducati's 'MyDucati' Smartphone app allowing riders to track their performance, manage service schedules, and even share their riding experiences with friends. It also let riders connect their smartphone to the bike, enabling hands-free calls, music control, and navigation prompts.

The resulting 2018 Ducati Panigale V4 was officially unveiled in late 2017 at Ducati's own World Premiere event in Milan, just prior to the EICMA show in November. It was launched to the world's press at the Circuit Ricardo Tormo in Valencia, Spain, in January of 2018, and arrived in dealer showrooms shortly after in early 2018.

At the press launch, Ducati official began their presentation by saying: "With a new engine, frame and electronics, the riding experience will be closer than ever to a race bike." They weren't wrong.

As before, following the model protocol Ducati had followed since the 996, three core models were offered: the base V4, the up-specced Panigale V4 S and, later, the smaller capacity, WSB-homologated, more track-orientated Panigale V4 R, each offering what Ducati claimed was a "unique blend of performance, technology, and design, catering to a wide range of enthusiasts and racing applications".

Both the base model and the S used the same 1103cc engine churning out a whopping 216bhp and 89.2lb-ft of torque. The smaller, racier 999cc R, meanwhile, produced 221bhp and 83.3lb-ft.

The base version also featured the following: fully adjustable 43mm Showa 'Big Piston' forks; a fully adjustable Sachs monoshock; Sachs steering damper; an electronics package with six-axis Inertial Measurement Unit (for measuring roll, yaw and pitch angles) including cornering ABS, traction control, slide control, wheelie control, launch control, up and down quickshifter, engine braking control, three riding modes (race, sport and street); a 16-litre aluminium tank; full LED headlight; new Brembo Stylema monobloc brake calipers: and Pirelli Supercorsa SP tyres with a whopping 200/60 at the rear!

The S version, which was bike tested at the Valencia press launch, went further still and added Öhlins suspension and steering damper via Öhlins 'Smart EC 2.0' semi-active system, which comprised Öhlins NIX-30 forks and TTX 36 shock absorber, lightweight aluminium forged wheels and lithium-ion battery, plus a lightweight cast magnesium alloy front sub frame.

To say the world's press were impressed would be an understatement. Britain's *MCN* reported: "After years of stunning V-twin sportsbikes, Ducati pulled off a masterstroke giving their top-of-the-range superbike a V4. It's genius – the perfect way to move on a V-twin concept that had reached the end of its development path while still allowing the bike the soul it needs."

They continued: "There is no doubting that this is a step forward from Bologna and they've made the most desirable sportsbike on the planet, with amazing, light handling, superb power delivery and the kind of top-end rush that skews your senses and tests your sheer ability to hold on. It's the real deal."

At the end of 2018, *MCN* also made the new Ducati Panigale V4 S its Bike of the Year.

Around the same time, the 998cc Panigale R arrived, producing as standard 215.1hp at 15,500rpm and 82.1lb-ft of torque at 12,000rpm, but with its race kit, this could reach up to 233hp. The R also featured a reworked frame and adjustable swingarm pivot, making it one of the most powerful street legal bikes out there.

Though a brilliant performer on road and track, Ducati's newcomer was still slightly slow to win on track – especially in WSB – against the more developed Kawasakis and Yamahas, which led to a series of

further improvements, plus some limited-edition special models.

In 2019 Ducati offered the Panigale V4 25th Anniversario, which commemorated 25 years of the Ducati 916. That year also saw the Panigale V4 Speciale, an exotic limited edition restricted to just 1,500 units which was described as a 'V4 S on steroids' and included all the S model options but with a few more luxury touches like adjustable footpads, an Alcantara-trimmed seat, and carbon mudguards. It also comes with a titanium exhaust and a race kit that bumps the power up to 223bhp.

BELOW: In superbike racing, MotoGP returnee Scott Redding (45), claimed its first British Superbike crown in 2019. DUCATI

In 2022 an even more exotic, ultra-lightweight Panigale V4 'Superleggera' version, continuing the tradition of the 1199 Superleggera, was also offered. That year also saw a further new variant, the Panigale V4 SP, while the core Panigale V4S also received a host of modest updates enhancing aerodynamics, ergonomics, and electronics to deliver a bike that's faster and more intuitive than ever.

The bike received a fresh look with improved aerodynamics, making it faster on the track while also being easier to handle. Updated engine mapping and torque management strategy resulted in new peak horsepower of 210bhp at 12,500rpm and 90.6 lb-ft of torque at 11,000rpm.

The superbike spec R gained a revised gearbox, as Ducati lengthened first, second, and sixth gears, with first now 11.6% longer, making it easier to handle tight corners, second gear 5.6% longer, which means better acceleration out of corners, and the longer sixth gear resulting in a higher top speed.

Its suspension also saw improvements, with a new Öhlins NPX 25/30 electronically controlled fork for a smoother ride

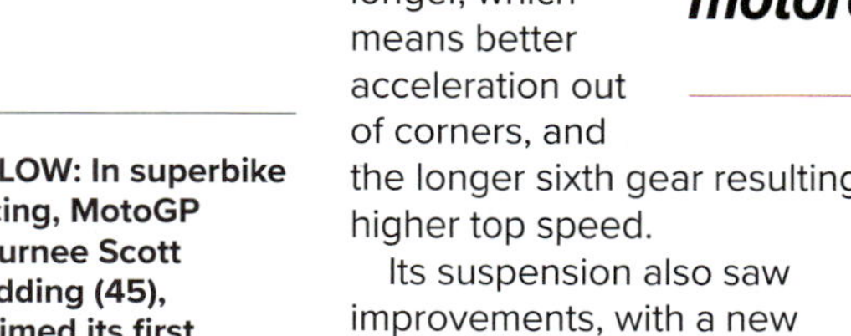

combined with an Öhlins TTX36 rear shock absorber and Öhlins steering damper.

And, by then, the Panigale V4 had more than proved its mettle on track, as well. In world superbikes, factory rider Spaniard Álvaro Bautista dominated the 2022 series with 16 wins, then went even further the following year with a massive 27 race wins.

In the British Superbike championship, MotoGP returnee Scott Redding took the Panigale V4 R to its first title in 2019, swiftly followed up by Josh Brookes in 2020, with a further crown going to Tommy Bridewell in 2023.

While for 2025, the Panigale V4, in all its forms, received its biggest makeover to date. New aero, clever mapping, revised gearbox ratios, refined rider aids, chassis upgrades, and new ergonomics all designed to not only make the new Panigale V4 S faster, but also friendlier on track.

As MCN found at its world press launch in September of 2024, stating: "With its flexy new frame, even more advanced electronics, clever braking system and a raft of detail upgrades, Ducati's new Panigale V4S has evolved into an ultra-polished track weapon. It'll lap faster than the outgoing model, for racing pros and track day regulars alike, and is as easy to ride as a brain-melting, 213bhp superbike can ever be. It's kinder on its tyres and its handling and stability stays consistent, even when grip fades away."

The latest Ducati Superbike may have come a long way since it first dominated the class with its 851/888 then 916, and may have ultimately had to sacrifice its traditional 90° L-twin engine layout, signature tubular steel trellis frame and even, with the 2025 model, its much-loved single-sided swing arm, but it remains the most loved, 'poster bike' superbike of all; the definitive example of an Italian motorcycle sporting exotica and the bike to beat on track.

At the end of 2025 Motorcycle News again gave the latest Ducati Panigale V4 S the Best Superbike award. Superbike commendations don't get much clearer than that. ■

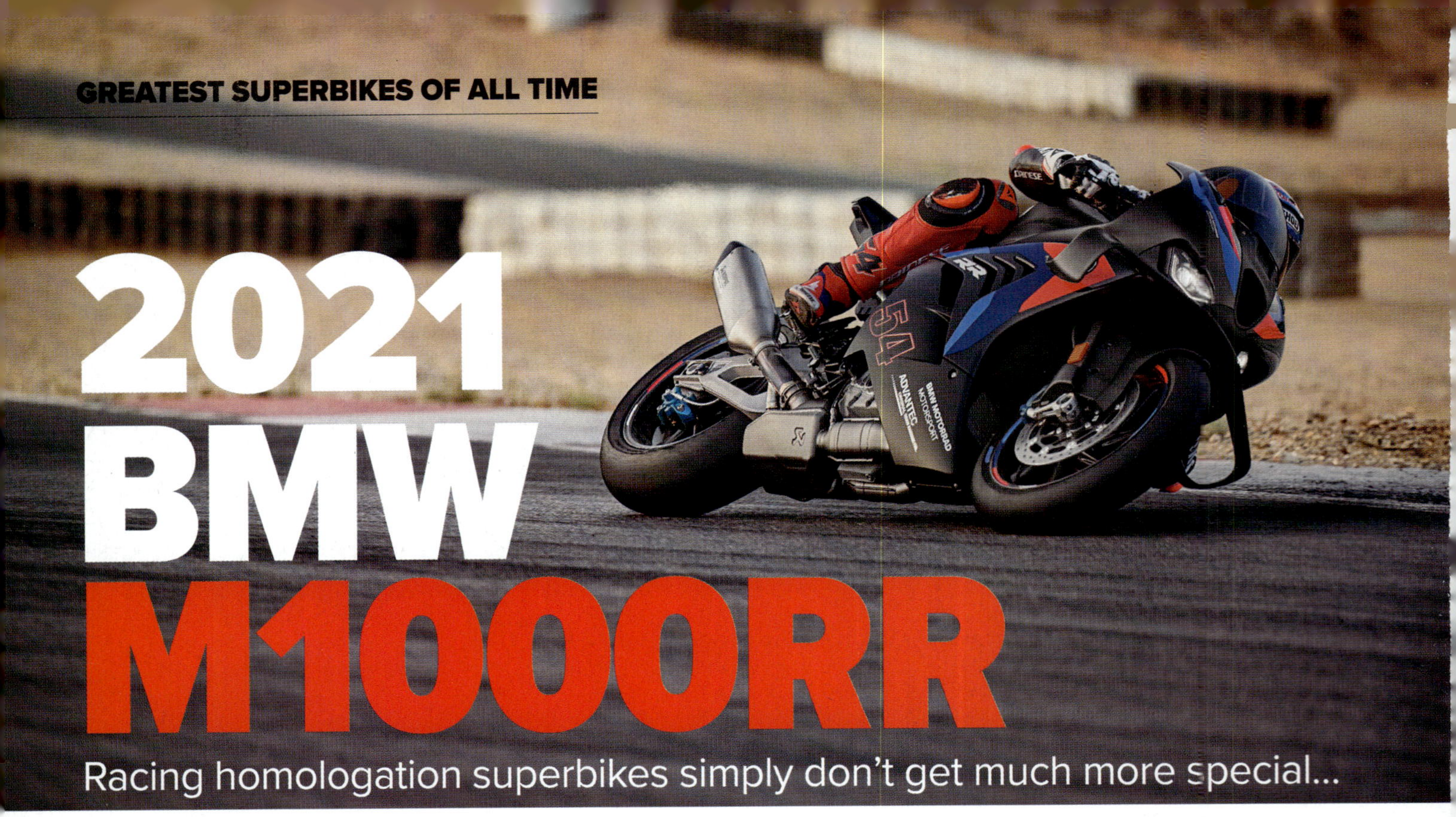

2021 BMW
M1000RR

Racing homologation superbikes simply don't get much more special...

By almost any parameter, BMW's outrageous M1000RR is the most extreme, potent and successful superbike of the mid-2020s.

The 'M-Sport', homologation special, racing version of what is already one of the class-leading superbikes (the S1000RR), BMW's 200bhp-plus beast is not only the reigning world superbike champion, but it has also become the go-to machine for the senior classes at the Isle of Man TT and is the lap record holder.

First launched in 2021, it has been updated twice since and is basically the S but with carbon everything, additional aero aids, updated suspension and brakes,

and a more tunable engine. As such, as a road bike (for, yes, the M1000RR is road legal), it offers little that's much use on the road over the already phenomenal S1000RR but costs nearly twice as much. As an ultimate, exclusive racer for the road, not even Ducati's equivalent, R version of its equally phenomenal Panigale, V4 comes close.

The M1000RR's engine is based on the 204bhp 999cc transverse four of the S1000RR, but has higher compression forged pistons, lighter, stronger valves and conrods, and the result is a phenomenal 212bhp at 14,500rpm with torque of 83lb-ft at 11,000rpm.

Although capable of nearly 200mph and able to reach a heady 140mph in second gear, its low-down delivery is still tractable and usable, which, if riding the M1000RR within legal speed limits on the street, seems pointless and irrelevant.

The M1000RR's chassis, cycle parts and aerodynamic bodywork are even wilder still. Although the frame is unchanged, the M's suspension, wheels and steering geometry were new. Mechanically adjustable Marzocchi suspension replaced the S's Sachs semi-active set-up and gave a firmer, more precise ride. Braking comprised special, blue-anodised, Nissin four-piston radial calipers working on thicker 320mm discs and the resulting power was phenomenal yet with plenty of finesse. There was also more rake and trail, and the wheelbase was slightly longer to add stability while lightweight

carbon fibre wheels were also available as an option.

But with the original 2021 version not delivering the race (and particularly WSB) success BMW craved, for 2023 the German marque went to the wind tunnel to improve the M1000RR's aerodynamics both for top speed and extra downforce, the result made asignificant difference and resulted in one of the wildest superbikes ever built.

The new, more bulbous, wider fairing increased claimed top speed from 190mph to 195mph by making it easier for the rider to get tucked in out of the wind on straights. Its larger 'wings' boosted downforce. A new carbon fibre front mudguard wrapped around the forks to further smooth airflow and it also had built-in air ducts to help cool its Nissin brakes. This BMW is now the fastest and the wildest-looking superbike so far built. ■

SPECIFICATIONS

Price new	£30,935
Engine	999cc liquid-cooled DOHC transverse four
Power	212bhp @ 14,500rpm
Torque	83lb-ft @ 11,000rpm
Frame	Aluminium twin spar
Suspension	45mm inverted telescopic forks (F), monoshock (R)
Brakes	2 x 320mm discs (F), 220mm disc (R)
Tyres	120/70 x 17 (F), 200/55 x 17 (R)
Dry weight	192kg
Top speed	190mph

ABOVE: With the standard but updated S1000RR not proving sufficient to win in world superbikes, BMW took things further in 2021 with the M1000RR. BMW

BELOW: Along with carbon bodywork, a more tunable engine and more conventional suspension, the M version had the most extreme 'aero' yet on a road bike. BMW